REPRINTED FROM THE JEWISH QUARTERLY REVIEW
NEW SERIES
VOLUME VII, NUMBER 1

CRESCAS ON THE PROBLEM OF
DIVINE ATTRIBUTES

BY

HARRY AUSTRYN WOLFSON

PHILADELPHIA
THE DROPSIE COLLEGE FOR HEBREW AND COGNATE LEARNING
1916

CRESCAS ON THE PROBLEM OF DIVINE ATTRIBUTES

By Harry Austryn Wolfson, Harvard University.

Prefatory Note.

It has been well said that in Arabic, and for that matter also in Jewish philosophy, the problem of Universals had never acquired, as it did later on in Scholasticism, the importance of an independent subject of inquiry. Still, the problem was not altogether unknown. Always latent, it occasionally cropped out in various philosophical discussions. We need only slightly penetrate below the surface of some controversies of the time in Metaphysics and Psychology to discover the lurking presence of the problem of Universals. For the true problem of Universals began with the rejection of Platonic Realism. Admitting with the Aristotelians that genera and species are mere products of the mind, the question was then raised as to what was the nature of those intellectual conceptions and their relation to the individual beings. It was this field of inquiry that proved a fertile ground for the crop of the many subtle and hardly distinguishable mediaeval theories of Universals. Now the same problem must inevitably appear whenever the mind perceives a distinction of a purely intellectual character in an object, and the solution of that problem will of necessity prove more difficult when, in addition to defining the nature of that intellectual distinction, we must at the same time safeguard the unity of the object. Thus, for instance, in the case of the soul, one and homogeneous, we may ask what is the relation between the essence and its faculties. And in the case of God, too, the absolutely simple, how are His attributes related to His essence?

It is as a problem of Universals in disguise that the problem of Attributes will be herein presented. I shall therefore forego the discussion of the lexicographical and exegetical aspect of the problem, namely, the enumeration of all the Attributes found in the Bible, and their explanation by Jewish philosophers, the object of this paper being to discuss the general principles underlying the problem and its solution. As part of a larger work upon the philosophy of Crescas, it deals more fully with that author. The two chapters devoted to him are intended both to present a constructive view of his theory and to serve as a commentary on his text. They are preceded by a chapter devoted to a general treatment of certain representative authors advisedly selected for their value as an introduction to the study of Crescas.

CHAPTER I

AN ANALYSIS OF THE PROBLEM AND SOME REPRESENTATIVE SOLUTIONS.

I.

THERE are four initial assumptions underlying the problem of divine attributes in mediaeval philosophy. The starting-point of the problem is the rationalistic attempt to invest the Scriptural predications of God with the validity of logical judgements. Then, a logical judgement is defined, after Aristotle, as having a double content, synthesizing as it does two distinct terms, of which one must be a universal, by bringing them together by one of the several relations obtaining between subject and predicate. In addition to these two assumptions, while Platonic Realism is not an essential prerequisite, the problem of attributes involves an anti-nominalistic conception of Universals. Finally, it follows Avicenna in identifying God with the metaphysical conception of necessary existence, whose simplicity by definition precludes from its being not only actual composition, but likewise any suggestion of noetic plurality and relativity. The question is then raised, How can we form a logical judgement about God without at the same time creating the anomaly of having the unrelatable Necessarily Existent brought into some logical relation with some predicate distinct from Himself? It is this apparent incompatibility of the formal interpretation of Biblical phraseology, the synthetic conception of a logical judgement, the anti-nominalistic view of universals, and the Avicennean definition of necessary existence that lies at the basis of the problem of attributes.

In Maimonides' treatment of Attributes we find a clear if not a formal statement of the problem. He sets out with a rationalistic definition of faith. Faith is not the correlative of reason, but rather the consummation of the reasoning process. Nor is it a mere attitude of mind, an inane state of consciousness; it is the comprehension of some objective reality. Furthermore, faith is not immediate comprehension or intuitive knowledge, the claim of mysticism, but it is resultant knowledge, the positive intellectual certainty arrived at after a process of ratiocinative reasoning. Faith thus being knowledge, derivative and logically demonstrable, the profession of faith must, therefore, have the force of logical judgements. They cannot be mere verbal utterance, mere irresponsible exclamations indicative but inexpressive of an attitudinal belief; they must be the embodiment of the conclusions of logical syllogisms, in which the premisses, though not stated, are assumed. Consequently the articles of faith, containing asseverations about the nature and being of God, based upon corresponding affirmations taken from the Scriptures, are perforce logical propositions conforming to all the regimens regulating such propositions.[1]

But a logical proposition must contain a synthesis of two distinct terms. Identity, contends Maimonides, is not a relation. A proposition in which the subject and predicate indicate one and the same thing is logically meaningless, for to assert that A is A is a mere tautology.[2] In this as well as in his subsequent elaborate statement of what he considers as real, logical relations, though at first sight he does not appear to do so, Maimonides is really following in the footprints of his Stagirite master. In order to show

[1] Cf. *Moreh*, I, 50. This identification of Faith with ratiocinative reasoning was common among certain classes of Moslem thinkers, and was not unknown to Jewish philosophers prior to Maimonides (cf. Kaufmann, *Attributenlehre*, p. 369, note 9. To Kaufmann's references may be added Ḥobot ha-Lebabot, I, 1). It seems to me that this view may be traced directly to Aristotle through Simplicius. In *De Caelo*, book I, chapter ii, Aristotle has the following statement: Διόπερ ἐξ ἁπάντων ἄν τις τούτων συλλογιζόμενος πιστεύσειεν. Upon this Simplicius comments as follows: Ἡ πίστις διττή ἐστιν, ἡ μὲν χωρὶς ἀποδείξεως ἀλόγως γινομένη, οἵαν τινὲς ἴσχουσι καὶ ἐπὶ τοῖς ἀτοπωτάτοις, ἡ δὲ μετὰ ἀπόδειξιν καὶ συλλογισμὸν ἀποδεικτικόν, ἥτις καὶ ἀσφαλής ἐστι καὶ ἀνέλεγκτος καὶ τῇ ἀληθείᾳ τῶν ὄντων συμπεφυκυῖα . . . κάλλιον δέ, οἶμαι, λέγειν, ὅτι ταῖς ἀποδεικτικαῖς ἀνάγκαις προσεῖναι παραινεῖ πανταχοῦ μέν, μάλιστα δὲ ἐν τοῖς περὶ τῶν θείων λόγοις τὴν ἀπὸ τῆς πίστεως συμπάθειαν, οὐ μόνον βεβαίωσιν τῆς ἀληθοῦς γνώσεως ἐμποιοῦσαν, ὅταν μετὰ τὴν ἀπόδειξιν ἐπιγένηται, ἀλλὰ καὶ τὴν πρὸς τὰ γνωστὰ ἕνωσιν, ἥτις ἐστὶ τὸ τέλος τῆς ἀνθρωπίνης μακρότητος (*Simplicii in Aristotelis De Caelo Commentaria*, ed. I. L. Heiberg, Berlin, 1894, p. 55).

[2] Cf. *Moreh*, I, 51.

this congruity, let us first give a genetic analysis of Aristotle's predicables.

It is from his classification of the Categories that Aristotle derives his predicables, for whatever other purpose that classification might have originally served in Aristotle's system, its function as expressing logical relations between subject and predicate is unquestionable.[3] When Aristotle, however, uses the categories in their restrictive application of predicables, instead of their common tenfold classification, he adopts their less current division into two, Substance and Accident.[4] Thus the predicate of a proposition may be either a Substance or an Accident. Neither of these, however, can be a particular. Two individual substances, denoting one and the same thing, cannot be related as subject and predicate. Likewise a definite accident cannot be predicated of a subject. 'John is John' and 'The table is *this definite red*' are not logical propositions. Conse-

---

[3] Whether the Categories were originally intended by Aristotle as logical or ontological divisions is a moot point (cf. Zeller, *Aristotle*, vol. I, p. 274, note 3; p. 275, note 1; Grote, *Aristotle*, vol. I, ch. iii). No question on this point, however, existed for the Arabic and Jewish philosophers. To them it was clear that the Categories were both logical and metaphysical, and are treated as such in the works of Alfarabi, Avicenna, and Algazali. Likewise in the Scholastic philosophy, the Categories had logical as well as metaphysical significance (cf. De Wulf, *Scholasticism Old and New*, p. 141).

[4] Averroes, in his paraphrase of Aristotle's Categories (ספר המאמרות לבן רש״ד), has the following classification: (1) Universal Substance (העצם הכולל), which is predicable of a subject but does not exist in it (ינשא על נושא ואיננו בנושא). (2) Particular accident (מקרה נרמז אליו), which exists in a subject but is not predicable of it (הוא בנושא ולא ינשא על נושא). (3) Universal accident (המקרה הכולל), which both exists in a subject and is predicable of it (ינשא על נושא והוא נ״כ בנושא). (4) Particular Substance (איש העצם), which neither exists in a subject nor is predicable thereof (לא ינשא על נושא ואיננו בנושא). Cf. Organon, *The Categories*, ch. ii.

quently, whether substance or accident, the predicables must be universals. Now, a universal substance may denote either the genus or the species of a thing, and a universal accident may be differentiated, with respect to its applicability, as more or less essential to the subject. In this way Aristotle derives his four predicables: genus, species, property, and accident, which, raised to five in Porphyry's 'Introduction' by the addition of 'specific difference', were referred to by mediaeval logicians as the five predicables.[5]

Herein, if I am not mistaken, we may find the origin of Maimonides' fivefold division of the possible relations between subject and attribute. Their difference in nomenclature is more apparent than real, and the process of their derivation from the Categories will be shown to tally with that followed by Aristotle. As already mentioned, Maimonides rejects identity as a logical relation, that is, the attributes cannot be taken as individual, first substances. What is now left is the alternative, that they must be either universal substances or universal accidents. In the words of Maimonides: 'It will now be clear that the attributes must be one of two things; either the essence of the object described—in that case it is a mere explanation of a name, &c.—or the attribute is something different from the object described' (*Moreh*, I, 51). This general twofold classification is now subdivided by Maimonides into five classes. Taking universal substance, from which the Aristotelians get genus, species, and specific difference, Maimonides

---

[5] Cf. *Intentions*, Logic. Algazali enumerates these five universals (הכוללים הנפרדים; הנפרדים החמשה) which may be predicated of a subject, namely, סוג, מין, הבדל, סגולה, מקרה. Sharastani likewise names the same five predicables: الفصل, لخاصّة, العرض العام, الجنم, النوع (ed. Cureton, p. 350).

divides it with respect to its function rather than with respect to its content, thus obtaining two classes, Definition and Part of Definition, for the combination of genus with species or with specific difference forms a definition, whence any one of these three may be properly called Part of Definition. Then again, taking universal accident, which by Aristotle is roughly subdivided into property and (general) accident, bearing upon the tenfold division of Categories, Maimonides divides it more minutely into three classes. The Categories of quantity and quality yield the relation of *Property*; those of Relation, Space, Time, Situation, and Possession are placed under the heading of *External Relations*, whereas the Categories of Action and Passion are designated by him as *Dynamic Relations*. Applying this theory of logical relations to the interpretation of divine attributes, Maimonides arrives at the following conclusion. The divine attributes cannot be identical with their subject, and, while they must be distinct, their relation to it must be equivalent to that of a Definition, Part of Definition, Property, External Relation or Action.[6]

If in the Biblical predications of God, as it has been shown, the attribute must be distinct from but related to the subject, the question then arises, By which of the five enumerated relations are they conjoined? To answer this question it must first be determined what is the nature of the subject of those attributes, or God, in so far as it is known by the proof for His Existence. Now, so much is known about the nature of God, that He is necessary existence, a term used by Avicenna, and corresponding to the Aristotelian Prime Mover. For just as Aristotle, taking motion as the starting-point of his physical inquiries, ulti-

[6] Cf. *Moreh*, I, 52.

mately arrived at the inevitable existence of a Prime Immovable Mover, so Avicenna, reflecting upon the nature of necessity and contingency, eventually concluded that there must be something that is Necessary Existence.[7] Whether Aristotle's Prime Mover should be identified with Avicenna's Necessary Existence is a controversial point which does not concern us now, and will be taken up elsewhere.[8] It is, however, clear that in his discussion of divine attributes Maimonides starts out with the Avicennean conception of Necessary Existence, the proof for which is incorporated by Maimonides within his various proofs for the existence of God.[9] Now, in the Avicennean application of the term, necessary or absolute existence means the negation of any cause whatsoever, the final as well as the efficient, the formal as well as the material. Thus the term Necessary Existence, negative in its original meaning with respect to causation, has ultimately acquired by the negation of all causes whatsoever the additional meaning of absolute simplicity and all which that connotes. The Necessarily Existent must, therefore, be absolutely simple, that is, its essence must exclude not only actual plurality, but metaphysical and epistemological plurality as well, being in no less degree impervious to the distinction between matter and form, genus and species, than to actual, physical disintegration and composition. Absolute simplicity, according to Avicenna, excludes the five possible kinds of plurality: (1)

[7] This will be fully discussed in a chapter on 'The Proofs for the Existence of God'. Cf. *Moreh*, II, 1, Third Argument.

[8] Cf. *ibid*.

[9] Cf. *Moreh*, II, 1, Third Philosophical Argument. This Avicennean argument is introduced by Maimonides as follows: 'This is taken from the words of Aristotle, though he gives it in a different form' (cf. Hebrew commentaries).

Actual plurality as that of physical objects; (2) noetic plurality as that of matter and form; (3) of subject and attribute; (4) of genus and species; and (5) of essence and existence.[10]

Absolute simplicity is thus the main fact known about necessary existence. And so, says Maimonides, when the necessarily existent is placed as the subject of a proposition, it cannot be related to its predicate by any of the first four of the five classes of relations enumerated. The reasons for that are variously stated by Maimonides, but it seems to me that they can all be classified under two headings: first, the implication of plurality; and second, the implication of similarity.[11]

[10] Cf. *Destruction of the Philosophers*, Disputation V.

[11] The classification of Maimonides' arguments into these two divisions is based upon the following facts: In chapters 50 and 51, Maimonides explicitly states that his ground for the rejection of attributes is to be found in the simplicity of the divine substance. In chapter 52, in his enumeration of the five classes of attributes, the first three are rejected for the following reasons: Definition because God has no previous causes (שהוא ית׳ אין לו סבות קודמות); Part of Definition because it would imply that in God essences were compound, and so it could have a definition which has been excluded on account of the implication of previous causation (cf. Afodi's commentary); Property because God is not a magnitude, He is not affected by external influences, He is not subject to physical conditions, and He is not an animate being. Now, all these reasons are in fact nothing but modifications of the chief reason, namely, the implication of the composition of the divine essence. They are thus summed up by Maimonides himself: 'Consequently, these three classes of attributes, describing the essence of a thing, or part of the essence, or a quality of it, are clearly inadmissible in reference to God, for they imply composition.' הנה אלו שלשה חלקים מן התארים, והם מה שיורה על מהות, או על איכות אחת נמצאת במהות, כבר התבאר המנעה בחקו יתעלה מפני שהם כלם מורים על הרכבה. The fourth class of attributes, that of external relation, are rejected by Maimonides not because they imply composition in the divine essence, but because a real external relation must not be assumed to exist between God and created beings. Why that must not be assumed, however, is explained

As for the first of these reasons, Maimonides restates Avicenna's conception of absolute simplicity. 'There cannot be any belief in the unity of God except by admitting that He is one simple substance, without any composition or plurality of elements; one from whatever side you view it, and by whatever test you examine it; not divisible into two parts in any way and by any cause, nor capable of any form or plurality either objectively or subjectively' (*Moreh*,

by him later on in chapter 56 on the ground that every relation implies similarity, the latter of which is inadmissible on independent grounds. Thus all the arguments against attributes may be reduced to the two classes I have named. In chapter 55 Maimonides advances the following four arguments against attributes: They imply (1) corporeality, (2) passiveness (הפעלות), (3) non-existence or potentiality (העדר, בכח), (4) similarity (דמוי). Here, too, the first three reasons are all reducible to the single reason that they imply composition. Likewise Crescas, in his restatement of Maimonides' arguments against positive attributes, classifies those arguments in the two parts I have mentioned. He says: 'If his contention were true that attributes must be negated on account of the inadmissibility of *composition* and of *relation or similarity* between God and others.' ומהם שאם היה החיוב שחייבו משלילת התארים אמתי להמנעות הרכבה ולהמנעות שום יחס ודמיון בינו ובין זולתו (מ"א, כ"נ, פ"א p. 25a). Abrabanel, however, reduces Maimonides' arguments to the following threefold classification: (1) on account of God's incorporeality, (2) on account of His eternity, and (3) on account of His unity (cf. commentary on the *Moreh*, I, 51): עיין שעשה הרב כאן באמונת התארים ג' בטולים הא' מצד חיות הש"י מסולק מן הגשמות, הב' מצד היותו קדמון, והג' מצד היותו אחד. Kaufmann approves of Abrabanel's classification (cf. *Attributenlehre*, p. 377, note 22).

Abraham Shalom has the following classification: (1) On account of the implication of plurality in God, (2) on account of the limitation of human understanding, and (3) on account of the implication of similarity or relation between God and His creatures (cf. *Neveh Shalom*, XII, i, iii). . . . האחת להיותו ית' מחויב המציאות אינו מורכב מחלקים . . . השנית היא מצדנו שהשב"ת לא יוכל לתאר הבב"ת באמת, השלישית . . . ואין לו ית' שום יחס ודמיון עם בריותיו. As will be noticed, the second of these three arguments is not found among the formal arguments of Maimonides.

Albo's classification of arguments against positive attributes (cf. *infra*, Chap. III, note 125) is not based upon Maimonides' text.

I, 51). Consequently, predicates taken in the sense of definition, part of definition, and accretion are inadmissible with respect to God. They all imply plurality in some sense or other. That accretive qualities are inadmissible goes without saying, since they imply that the subject is composed of external attributes inherent in or adherent to its substance. The inadmissibility of a definition or its parts is not so obvious. To affirm of God attributes which, like the parts of a definition, are merely descriptive of the substantial essence without implying the composition of the substance with anything unessential, would at first sight seem to be quite appropriate. That too, however, is inadmissible, for while the parts of a definition do not imply the composition of the defined substance with something external thereto, there is still the implication that the substance itself is composed, as it were, of two essences, the particular and the universal. It is here that Maimonides' theory of universals comes into play. For nominalism, it may be inferred, Maimonides had the same abhorrence as for logical verbalism.[12] There is the ring of a genuine

[12] It is generally stated that Arabic as well as Jewish philosophers were all nominalists (cf. Munk's *Mélanges*, p. 327), 'Les Péripatéticiens arabes, comme on le pense bien, devaient tous professer le nominalisme d'une manière absolue, et plusieurs d'entre eux se prononcent à cet égard dans les termes les plus explicites'. Among the last referred to he includes, in note 1, also Maimonides, who in *Moreh*, III, 18 states that 'species have no existence except in our own minds' (שאין חוץ לשכל שום נמצא אבל המין נשאר הכלליות דברים שכליים). Cf. also Kaufmann's *Attributenlehre*, p. 379, note 29, 'Was aber Maimûni's Stellung in dem Streite über die Universalien angeht, so bekennt er sich als Aristoteliker zum strengen Nominalismus und läugnet entschieden deren Realität'. Of course, to say that one is a nominalist does not mean anything unless it is definitely explained how the term nominalism is employed. With regard to Maimonides it must be positively stated that his nominalism did not go further than the rejection of Platonic realism. His statement to the effect that the universals are in

feeling of contempt, characteristic of his rationalistic temper of mind, in his sneers at a *flatus vocis*, at 'things that are only said, existing only in words, not in thought, much less in reality' (*Moreh*, I, 51). Platonic realism, claiming the reality of ideas apart from the world of sense, had been discredited with the advent of Aristotelianism long before the age of Maimonides.[13] In various works on Logic and Metaphysics the absurdity of such a conception is pointed out without even recording a dissenting opinion. Conceptualism, to be sure, had found adherents among Arabic philosophers, but Maimonides, no less than Avicenna, evidently rejected that view. To him the assertion of ideal without real existence could have no meaning. Subjective reality, if it means anything, could merely mean that the reality affirmed has only a verbal significance. It is undoubtedly with reference to Conceptualism that Maimonides points out the meaninglessness of ideal existence and the incongruity in 'the assertion of some thinkers, that the ideas, i.e. the universals, are neither existent nor nonexistent'[14] (*Moreh*, I, 51). What Maimonides, as a follower of Avicenna and in common with all his contemporaries, conceived of universals is that they have both ideal and real existence. Universals, to be sure, exist in the mind, but the human mind does not *invent* them out of nothing.

mind does not commit him to anything definite. That very same statement had been used by Averroes in quite a different sense. The question is, as we shall see, how much in mind they are, and this can only be determined by analysis of such problems where the existence of universals is involved. From our analysis of Maimonides' theory of Attributes it will be gathered that it can hardly be said of him that he was a nominalist 'd'une manière absolue' or that he declared his adherence 'zum strengen Nominalismus'.

[13] Cf. Munk's *Mélanges*, p. 327.

[14] Cf. Munk's and Friedländer's notes on this passage; Munk's *Mélanges* pp. 327 and 328, n. 1; Kaufmann, *Attributenlehre*, p. 379, n. 29.

What the mind does is only to *discover* them in the multifarious individuals. For prior to the rise of individual beings the universals exist in the mind of God as independent entities, and they remain as such even when they enter upon plurality in material form, though their presence in the individuals is indiscernible except by mental activity.[15] Consequently even in essential attributes, as those which form a definition, there must necessarily be the implication of plurality in the subject. For the definition is not merely a verbal description of the essence, the latter being in itself one and uniform, but, as said Avicenna, the parts of the definition are the predicates of the thing defined. And so, since genus and specific difference are real in a certain sense, and not mere words, the thing defined by its genus and specific difference must be composite in so far as that genus and specific difference are real. That composition, to be sure, would only be mentally discernible, but still it would be inconsistent with the conception of absolute simplicity.

Let us now assume that the universals predicated of God are neither essential nor accidental qualities, but rather external relations between God and His creatures. This interpretation of attributes though sanctioned by the traditional philosophy of his time[16] is rejected by Maimonides

---

[15] Cf. Avicenna's *Eš-Šefah*, translated by M. Horten under the title of *Die Metaphysik Avicenna's*, Part V, ch. 1; De Boer's *Philosophy in Islam* (Eng. tr.), p. 135; Prantl's *Geschichte der Logik*, vol. II, in his exposition of Alfarabi, pp. 305-6, and in that of Avicenna, pp. 347 and 384, especially note 181; Carra de Vaux, *Avicenne*, pp. 224-5.

[16] In his *Intentions of the Philosophers* (*Metaphysics*, Part III, On the Attributes), Algazali restates Avicenna's interpretation of divine attributes as (1) negations (שלילה) and (2) relations (צרוף). Under relations he includes both what Maimonides calls 'external relations' and what he calls 'actions'. The same view is repeated by him in his *Destruction of the Philosophers*, Disputation V. Among Jewish philosophers, Abraham Ibn

as inadequate. In their ultimate analysis he says all such relations may be shown either to have no meaning at all, or, if they do have any meaning, to imply similarity between God and other beings. Relations are fourfold: temporal, spatial, reciprocative, and comparative. God, being incorporeal, cannot have any temporal or spatial relations. Again, His self-sufficiency and absolute independence precludes the relation of reciprocity, for His creativeness, His knowledge, and His beneficence are absolutely independent of the created, known and beneficiary objects. Finally, a relation of comparison exists only when things compared involved a specific identity, and differ only in individual diversity. White and green on that account are incomparable terms, even though they are identical as to their genus colour. Nor are they related terms; they are rather correlative and antithetical, their diversity being specific. God cannot, therefore, be compared with and related to other beings with respect to any predicate affirmed of Him, since all His predicates are indicative of attributes which are identical with essence, and hence absolute and immutable.[17] Nor can we claim that the attributes are some kind of subjective external relations, for every relation must imply a similarity.[18] If two things are related they are in so far

---

Daud, in his *Emunah Ramah* (Book II, Principle III), permits the use of relational attributes. In fact Maimonides was the first to distinguish between external relations and actions, and while permitting the latter to proscribe the former. Cf. *infra*, Chap. II.

[17] Cf. *Moreh*, I, 52.

[18] Cf. *ibid.* 'Besides, if any relation existed between them, God would be subject to the accident of relation, and although that would not be an accident to the essence of God, it would still be, to some extent, a kind of accident.' To which Shem-tob adds the following explanation: 'If any relation was affirmed of Him, even though an unreal relation, God would be subject to the accident of relation, that is to say, God would have to

similar, and so if a subjective relation means anything there must also be some meaning to subjective similarity. But there can be no similarity between God and other beings; hence, there cannot be any relation between them. For the preclusion of similarity Maimonides advances no arguments.[19] He refers to it as a well-accepted principle which seems to be exclusively based upon Scriptural inferences.

Of the five logical relations originally postulated by Maimonides there is now only one left, the dynamic, which has not been disqualified as a possible explanation of divine attributes. This is retained by Maimonides. The divine attributes are dynamic relations, that is to say, they are descriptive of the operating process of the activity rather than of the qualification therefor.[20] That the assertion of

resemble some other creature, even though that relation would not be an accident added to His essence.' ואם יתיחס לו שום יחס אפילו שיהיה בלתי אמתי ישינהו מקרה היחס, והוא שיהיה דומה לשום נברא אעפ"י שאינו מקרה נוסף עליו. Shem-tob's explanation is probably based upon chapter 56, wherein Maimonides elaborately explains the interdependence of relativism and similarity.

[19] For the negation of similarity Maimonides advances no argument except that of authority. 'Another thing likewise to be denied in reference to God is similarity to any existing being. This has been generally accepted [even by the Mutakallemim, cf. Shem-tob's commentary], and is also mentioned in the books of the Prophets; e. g. "To whom, then, will you liken me?" [Isa. 40. 25].' ומה שראוי בהכרח שירוחק ממנו נ"כ הדמוי לשום דבר מן הנמצאות, וזה דבר כבר הרגיש בו כל אדם [אפילו המדברים, שם טוב] וכבר נלה בספרי הנביאים בהרחקת הדמוי ואמר ואל מי תדמיון אל. Though later on he adds, 'It is necessary to demonstrate by proof that nothing can be predicated of God that implies similarity' (ראוי בהכרח להרחיק ממנו במופת ... מה שיביא לדמיון), he does not, however, state the proof for this, except that by inference he maintains that similarity must imply a real and not only an external relation. Cf. Ḥobot ha-Lebabot, I, 7 וששי.

[20] Cf. *Moreh*, I, 52. 'I do not mean by *its actions* the inherent capacity for a certain work, as is expressed in *carpenter, painter*, or *smith*, for these

activities implies no plurality in the subject is apparent, for
activities denote some external relation of the subject to its
environment. In point of fact, most of the Arabic as well
as Jewish philosophers do not treat activities as a special
logical relation; but, including them together with space
and time under the heading of External Relation, admit
them all as divine attributes.[21] The separation of activities
as a distinct class of logical relations is effected here by
Maimonides because of his rejection of non-dynamic external
relations on account of their implication of similarity. It
might be questioned, indeed, Why should not activities, too,
be excluded on account of similarity? As we shall see
later on, this difficulty has not been allowed to pass un-
challenged by Crescas.[22] For our present purpose, it suffices
to state that dynamic relations, according to Maimonides,
imply no plurality in the subject, and consequently the
divine attributes must be interpreted as designations of
activities.

There are, however, two points with regard to dynamic
attributes which need some further explanation. First,
while it is true that the assertion of any action in itself does
not necessarily imply the existence of an accidental quality
in the subject, the assertion of many diverse actions, it would
seem, must of necessity be accounted for by some kind of
diversity in its source, the subject. Second, while some
of the Scriptural attributes, as knowledge, can be easily
turned into actions, there are others, as life, which do not
appear to have any active implication whatsoever. As to

belong to the class of qualities which have been mentioned above; but
I mean the action the latter has performed. We speak, e. g. of Zaid, who
made this door, built that wall, wove that garment.'

[21] Cf. *supra*, note 16.   [22] Cf. *infra*, Chap. II.

the first, Maimonides maintains that the various activities affirmed of God are in reality emanating as a single act from the divine essence, its manifold ramification being only apparent.[23] As a single ray of light emanating from a luminous object, by striking through a lens breaks into many rays, so the single act of God becomes diversified by striking the lower strata of reality. One in essence, its manifoldness is due merely to the various aspects in which the divine action appears to the human eyes. As for the second point, Maimonides shows inductively how all the Biblical predications have active implications.[24] To do that, however, there was no need for him to go through the entire list of attributes found in the Bible. Most of them had been admitted by the Attributists themselves to be actions;[25] some of them were a matter of controversy. There were only four, which, unable to interpret as actions, the Attributists considered as essential attributes. These four—life, knowledge, will, power—are shown by Maimonides, in their ultimate analysis, to be actions, and one single action withal.

While the controversial attributes of life, knowledge, will, and power are interpreted by Maimonides as dynamic relations, the attributes of existence, unity, and eternity are admitted by him to be nothing but static.[26] And yet they are not attributes; they are absolutely identical with the divine essence. In created beings, to be sure, Maimonides, following Avicenna and the early Arabic philosophers, declares existence and unity to be adjoined to the essence;

[23] Cf. *Moreh*, I, 53. [24] Cf. *ibid*.
[25] Cf. Abrabanel's quotation from Averroes in his commentary on the *Moreh*, I, 53.
[26] Cf. *Moreh*, I, 57.

in the case of God, however, they are the essence itself.[27] But if you argue that since identity is not a relation, the proposition that 'God is existent' or that 'God is one' would be tautological, the answer is that the predicates in this case, though positive in form, are negative in meaning; that logically 'God is existent' is equivalent to 'God is not absent', and 'God is one' to 'God is not many'. And having once stated this new solution of the problem of attributes, reverting now to those predicates he has previously interpreted as actions, Maimonides declares that even those may be taken as static and interpreted as negations.[28]

The admissibility of negative attributes, which is at first stated by Maimonides as an incontestable fact, is afterwards subjected to a searching examination.[29] In an elaborate discussion, illustrated by concrete examples, he clearly points out the distinction between the knowledge of a determinate and of an indeterminate object. Negative attributes as well as positive ones define and limit the object of knowledge, but they do so in different ways. Positive attributes limit the number of all the possible conjectures about an unknown object by singling out a few which constitute its essence; negative attributes eliminate all those conjectures by showing that neither one nor all of them constitute its essence. The former, therefore, is a characterization of the object; the latter is only a circumscription and individualization thereof. As the divine

[27] Cf. *Moreh*, I, 57, and *infra*, Chap. II.

[28] This may be deduced from the following passage: 'Consequently God exists without existence. Similarly He lives without life, knows without knowledge, is omnipotent without omnipotence, and is wise without wisdom' (*ibid.*).

[29] Cf. *Moreh*, I, 58.

essence is without determinations and is unknowable, negative attributes are permissible, whereas positive ones are proscribed.

In this statement of Maimonides' negative interpretation of attributes I have followed the traditional view. Maimonides, according to this, attaches no significance whatsoever to the positive form of those attributes which are interpreted by him negatively.[30] 'God is existent' means 'God is not absent', the positive form of the former proposition being absolutely meaningless. This interpretation of Maimonides, though prevalent and widespread, does not, however, seem to me quite correct. I think he attributes some logical significance to the positive form of judgements about God as well as to their negative contents. Let us just briefly restate the problem which Maimonides was called upon to solve. His main problem was not whether God possesses any essential attributes. That assumption was ruled out of court by the absolute simplicity of God on the one hand, and by the Avicennean theory of universals on the other; his main problem concerned the meaning of the logical predicate affirmed of God. These predicates, not being universals, and of necessity identical with the divine essence, must consequently form tautological propositions. It is this avoidance of a tautology, I think, that Maimonides aims at in his negative interpretation of attributes. The divine predicates, he says, though expressing a relation of identity with the subject, are not tautological, for the affirmation of identity has an emphatic meaning, implying as it does the negation of diversity. 'God is existent' is, to be sure, equivalent to

---

[30] Cf. Gersonides' criticism of Maimonides in *Milḥamot*, III, 3, which is quoted below in note 54.

the affirmation that 'God is God', but still even the latter proposition may be logically justified if it means to emphasize that 'God is not Man'. Similarly 'God is existent' emphasizes the negation of absentness. The justification of identity as a logical relation by means of its emphatic use, is found in the Logic of Alfarabi.[31] Thus, the positive forms of predicates are not altogether useless according to Maimonides. And this is exactly what he means by saying that the divine predicates are homonymous terms. Not being universal, and expressing a relation of identity, divine predicates are absolutely unrelated with similarly sounding predicates describing other beings. In the following statements of Maimonides, 'God exists without existence, lives without life', &c., we clearly see that 'God is existent' does not merely mean that 'God is not absent', but what it means is that God is existent with an existence of His own, identical with His own essence. To affirm this is to emphasize the negation of existence used as a universal term.

If, as we have just said, by negative attributes Maimonides means that the divine predicates affirm a relation of identity, emphasizing the negation of a non-identical relation, it follows that the term *negative* must have been used by Maimonides in some special sense. By negative attributes he does not mean that the proposition in which a predicate is affirmed of God is negative in quality. He means that although the proposition itself is positive in quality, the predicate is to be understood to have a negative prefix.

---

[31] 'In a proposition like the following, the predicate and subject can both be individual: "The one who is sitting is Reuben"' (Alfarabi, *Book on Syllogism*). הנשוא יכל לחיות נ״כ אישי עם הנושא אישי במשפט הזה : זה (Brit. Mus. Harley 5523, p. 71 החקש בספר (אלפרבי ראובן הוא היושב.

Thus, 'God is one' is not to be convertible into 'God is not many', but the term 'one' must be taken to mean 'not-many', the quality of the proposition as a whole remaining unaltered. In order fully to appreciate this distinction, let us briefly restate what Aristotle had said about the quality of propositions. There is, he points out, a distinction between a proposition wherein the negative particle modifies the copula, and that wherein it modifies the subject or the predicate. The former is a negative proposition, the latter is an affirmative proposition with an indefinite subject or predicate, as the case may be.[32] A negative proposition expresses the privation of the subject of one of two alternative qualities, thus always implying its possession of the other; an affirmative proposition with an indefinite predicate expresses the exclusion of the subject of a certain class of qualities which are irrelevant to its nature. The latter kind of proposition is said to express what Kant would call an infinite or limiting judgement, as is to be distinguished from a negative judgement, as the proposition 'The soul is not-mortal' is to be distinguished in meaning from that of 'The soul is not mortal'.[33] It is in the sense of the Aristotelian indefinite predicate that Maimonides uses the expression 'negative attribute', the negative particle being hyphenated with the predicate, thus excluding the subject not only from the stated predicate, but also from implication of its antithesis. This seems to me to constitute the significance of the following passage: 'Even the negative attributes must not be found and applied to God, except in the way in which, as you know, sometimes an attribute is negatived with reference to a thing, although that attribute

[32] Cf. *Organon*, On Interpretation, ch. x, and *Metaphysics*, IV, 22.
[33] Cf. Sigwart's *Logic*, vol. I, ch. iv.

can naturally never be applied to it in the same sense ; as, e.g. we say, "The wall is not seeing"' (*Moreh*, I, 58). It is quite evident that we never say 'the wall is not seeing', except in the sense of 'the wall is not-seeing'.[34]

The rejection of positive essential attributes and the admission only of negatives, which is tantamount to a confession of our ignorance of the divine essence, gives rise to the question whether thereby it would be possible at all to mark any gradation in human knowledge of the divine being. But that one's comprehension of God is commensurable with one's intellectual and moral virtues is a postulate of both reason and tradition.[35] In answer to this difficulty, Maimonides maintains that knowledge arrived at by negation is as capable of increase as knowledge attained by determination. The negative interpretation of attributes, since it has been explained to express the affirmation of the relation of identity emphasizing the negation of irrelevant qualities, has a double meaning. While excluding God from knowable universal qualities, the attributes affirm of Him some unknowable qualities, peculiar to Himself, and identical with His essence. When we exclude God from

---

[34] That this is what has been meant by Maimonides is quite clear from his statement in his *Milot ha-Higayon*, which asserts that it cannot be said that 'The wall is blind'. ולא יתואר בשם ההעדר כי אם אשר מטבעו שימצא לו חקין ההוא הנוכחי להעדר ההוא, כי אנחנו לא נאמר בכתל שהוא סכל ולא עור ולא אלם (מלות ההגיון, שער י"א). Narboni in his commentary on the *Moreh* calls this kind of negation, referred to here by Maimonides, 'general' or 'absolute' (והמשלחת), a term which has been adopted by the modern commentators, as Munk, Kaufmann, and Friedländer, in explaining the text. כבר ידעת ממה שקראת מלאכת ההגיון כי השלילה שני מינים: האחת השלילה המיוחדת [כמו בלעם אינו רואה] .... והשני השלילה המשלחת ... [כמו הכתל אינו רואה]. Cf. *Metaphysics*, IV, 22.

[35] Cf. *Moreh*, I, 59.

the attribute of ordinary existence, for example, at the
same time we affirm that He exists with an existence of
His own. God, by virtue of His absolute perfection in
every sense, has an infinite number of aspects in His
essence ; and had we only the means of doing so, we should
be able to express them all in human language. But on
account of the unknowability of the divine essence, we can
express none of its infinite aspects in positive terms ; we
can only indirectly hint at them by negating of Him our
own knowable perfections. Not only must our affirmations
of divine infinite perfections be indirect, they must also be
limited in number, since the knowable human perfections
that are negated of Him are finite in number. This limitation on our part involves a serious difficulty. For in the
conditional reality of the world we know there is always
a line of demarcation between what is always already
actually known and what is actually unknown but is knowable. In so far as we are cognizant of conditional reality
we are able to distinguish God from the world, the absolute
from the conditional. By negations, we exclude Him from
the known quantity of perfections and indirectly affirm of
Him a corresponding number of unknowable divine perfections. Beyond that boundary line, which marks off that
which is known from that which is unknown in the knowable
world, God and the world appear to us to merge together,
and though we do not say so, since we are unable to negate
it, we assume as it were that God possesses all the knowable
qualities of the undiscovered part of reality. But this
limitation which springs from our disability varies with
each individual. The boundary line between the known
and the unknown in the knowable world shifts backward
and forward in accordance with one's own intellectual

attainments. To the more informed the known part of reality is greater than to the less informed. The former hence can directly deny more knowable human perfections of God, and indirectly affirm more unknowable divine perfections than the latter. Thus, while neither possesses positive knowledge of the divine essence, their indirect knowledge of God varies widely. Furthermore, the realm of the knowable has not yet been completely laid bare, and, consequently, as our knowledge of conditional existence has before it ample opportunity of growth and expansion, so our knowledge of absolute existence of God might gradually draw nearer to perfection. Thus by means of the quantitative distinction in the knowledge of conditional reality between different individuals, and by means of the multiplicability of that knowledge in each individual, Maimonides conceives the possibility of a rising scale in men's knowledge of the divine essence.[36]

Maimonides' theory of attributes is typical rather than original. None before him, to be sure, had analysed the problem so minutely and comprehensively as he, but his constructive view does not differ from those of his predecessors. Negative and dynamic interpretations of divine attributes had been the common stock-in-trade of Arabic and Jewish philosophers ever since Philo.[37] As thus far noticed, Maimonides departs from the commonly accepted view solely by differentiating between actions and external relations and his disqualification of the latter. Again, with the exception of the naïve theologians, referred to by

---

[36] Cf. *ibid.* While I have given here a rather free interpretation of the chapter, I hope I have remained true to its spirit.

[37] Cf. Munk, *Guide*, I, ch. 58, p. 238, note 1, and Kaufmann's *Attributenlehre*, p. 481.

Maimonides himself, none of the rational thinkers admitted the propriety of accretive attributes. The discussion was focused mainly on the so-called essential attributes, that is, the universal predicates which enter into the formation of definitions. Thus the problem of attributes runs parallel to that of universals and to that of the nature of logical propositions. We have seen how all these problems converge in the theory of Maimonides. Taking universals to be present as something distinct within individuals, and finding the predication of such universals to be inconsistent with the absolute simplicity of God; believing that a logical proposition must affirm a real relation unless that affirmation is emphatic, he was forced to declare all divine predicates to be relations of identity emphasizing a negation. In his own language, the divine predicates are homonymous terms, having nothing in common with terms of the same sound. Following the same analysis of the problem, we shall now expound several other representative theories of attributes. Algazali's criticism of Avicenna will be taken as our starting-point, after which we shall discuss Averroes and two of his Jewish followers, Gersonides and Moses Halavi, and finally we shall give a rather full account of an entirely new view proposed by Crescas on this subject of divine attributes.

II

Algazali's approach to the solution of the problem is unique in its kind. He dares what nobody else before him had ever thought of doing, to impugn the Avicennean definition of necessary existence. Does necessary existence preclude noetic plurality? that is the main burden of his inquiry. His answer is in the negative. The primary meaning of necessary existence, he contends, is the absence of efficient causation.³⁸ The Avicennean proof for the conception itself, indeed, merely establishes the fact of an ultimate terminus to the interlacing chain of cause and effect. That terminus is necessary in the sense that its springing into being had not been effected by the operation of a pre-existent agent. The phrase *necessary existence*, therefore, means nothing but primary existence, the term *necessary* signifying in this phrase a description of the spatial and temporal relation of a certain being in a series of causally interrelated entities rather than a qualitative determination of the nature of that being. If we are now asked, Can the necessarily existent be composite? the answer would depend upon the circumstance whether the composition in question would be subversive to the uncon-

---

³⁸ Cf. *Destruction of the Philosophers*, Disputation VII. 'The source of error and blunder in all this discussion is to be found in the expression "necessary existence". But to us the expression seems to be irrelevant, for we do not admit that the proof for necessary existence establishes anything except the existence of something eternal which had not been preceded by an efficient agent. If that is its meaning, the expression "necessary existence" must be dropped out of discussion. You must state your contention plainly, that it is impossible that there should be plurality and distinction in an eternal existence which had not been preceded by an efficient agent. But this you will be unable to prove.' ומקד השבוש וההמעורה בכל זה הוא מליצת מחוייב המציאות, ולכן לא תזכר ולא תפקד, כי אנחנו לא נודה שהראיה תורה על מחוייב המציאות אלא א״כ יהיה הנרצה בו קדמון שאין לו פעל, ואם היה זה הנרצה, תעוב נא מליצת מחוייב המציאות, ויאמר בפירוש שהוא מן השקר שימצא רבוי והבדל בנמצא קדמון שאין לו פעל, וזה אין לכם ראיה עליו (הפלת הפילוסופים, שאלה ז׳).
The same argument recurs in Disputations V, VI, VIII, IX, and X.
This seems to me to be the central argument made by Algazali. Curiously enough, De Boer, in his *Der Widerspruch der Philosophie nach al-Gazali*, does not even mention it. Neither is it mentioned in Carra de Vaux's *Gazali*, ch. II, where he discusses the latter's theory of attributes.

ditional existence of the being, unconditional in the sense
that it is not grounded in an efficient cause. If the com-
positeness be not subversive to such unconditional being,
then the necessarily existent may be composite. By means
of the conception of necessary existence so stated, Algazali
proceeds to show that the necessarily existent, according
to Avicenna's own definition, might be composed of matter
and form,[39] of substance and attribute;[40] it might also be
defined in terms of genus and difference;[41] and, finally,
that it might also have existence superadded to its essence.[42]
Indeed, Algazali goes even farther. The original conception
of necessary existence does not, he holds, preclude the
duality of absolutely existent beings.[43] Unity, simplicity,
and incorporeality are all unwarranted by necessary existence. It is only by vitiating the primary meaning of the
term, by extending the proof for the absence of any
efficient cause whatsoever, that necessary existence had
come to be used by philosophers in the sense of absolute
simplicity; and, again, it is by a kind of vicious intellec-
tualism which reasons from the conception of absolute
simplicity rather than from the conception of necessary
existence, that the philosophers had erroneously inferred
the necessity of the first unconditionally existent being as
one, simple, undefinable, and unrelatable.

[39] Cf. Disputation IX: בלאותם מהעמיד ראיה על שהראשון אינו נשם.

[40] Cf. Disputation VI: בהסכימם על שקרות קיום המדע, והיכלת, והרצון, להתחלה ראשונה.

[41] Cf. Disputation VII: בבטל אמרם שמציאות הראשון אי״א שישתתף עם זולתו בסוג ויובדל ממנו בהבדל.

[42] Cf. Disputation VIII: בבטל אמרם שמציאות הראשון פשוט כלומר הוא מציאות גמור ואין מהות ולא אמתות יוצרף המציאות עליהם.

[43] Cf. Disputation V: בבאור לאותם מהעמיד ראיה על שהאל אחד ושא״א להניח שני מחויבי המציאות כל אחד אין עלה לו.

Algazali's argument against Avicenna's conception of necessary existence is based upon the latter's use of the term 'possibility'. Possibility, according to mediaeval Jewish and Arabic logicians, has two meanings. In the first place, it applies to a thing which without any cause whatsoever may by its own nature come or not come into being. This is the real and primary meaning of possibility. In the second place, the term applies to a thing which cannot come into existence save through an external cause, in the sense that in so far as the thing is dependent upon a cause, with respect to itself it is only possible, since its existence is determined by the presence or absence of that cause. This is the unreal and derivative meaning of possibility.[44] Real possibility is thus the antithesis of impossibi-

---

[44] Moses Halavi, in his Treatise 'On the First Mover', discussing Avicenna's proof for necessary existence, makes the following comment: 'The term possibility is not used here in the sense in which it is used in the Logic, namely, that which may or may not exist. But we must understand that the expression of having by itself only possible existence is another way of saying that it owes its existence to something else. Necessity and impossibility are not, therefore, its antitheses. For the existence which accrues to some external cause may sometimes be necessary and sometimes not. In both cases, however, we call it possible by itself, by which we mean that of whatever nature the existence in reality is, it is due to some external cause.' To this the Hebrew translator adds the following note: 'In general, he [i.e. Avicenna] does not mean by possibility that whose antithesis is necessity, but that whose antithesis is self-sufficiency.'

"וזה שהוא לא נשא מלת האפשר בכאן על הבנתה במלאכת ההגיון, והוא אשר יתחייב לו אפשר שלא ימצא אלא ידענו שאמרנו בכאן אפשר המציאות לעצמותו הוא מליצה מק[נין] המציאות מהזולת, והתברר פה והעדרו בלתי נוכחיים, כי לפעמים יהיה המציאות הנקנה מהזולת הכרחי, ולפעמים לא יהיה כן. ונאמר בשני ענינים שהוא אפשר המציאות לעצמותו, רצוני, שמציאותו איזה דרך היה מדרכי המציאות נקנה מזולתו" המעתיק העברי הוסיף בכאן על הנליון: "ובכלל אין כוונתו כאן במלת אפשרי אשר מקבילו ההכרח, אלא אשר מקבילו ההסתפקות בעצמו".

lity and necessity; unreal possibility is the antithesis of self-sufficiency. Now, in his proof of the existence of God, Avicenna uses the term possibility in its unreal meaning.[45] From the observation that all existences, sublunary as well as translunary, are with respect to themselves only possible, on account of the presence of an external cause, he concludes that there must be a prime cause which is necessary even with respect to itself. In what sense, according to Avicenna, must that prime cause be necessary with respect to itself? Certainly in the same sense as that in which the other existences are possible, namely, with respect to external causation. Consequently his proof for the presence of a necessarily existent being merely establishes the self-sufficiency of that being; that is, its independence with respect to external causation, without, however, disproving its dependence upon internal causation. Hence, Algazali's criticism against Avicenna's identification of necessary existence with absolute simplicity.

That Algazali's criticism is incontrovertible is generally admitted. In his *Destruction of the Destruction* Averroes refutes Algazali's contentions not by justifying Avicenna, but by showing that Avicenna is misrepresenting the philo-

---

[45] Cf. Averroes' *Destruction of the Destruction*, Disputation X. 'It was Avicenna's intention to have his distinction between possibility and necessity correspond to the philosophers' view of existences, for according to all the philosophers the celestial spheres are said to be necessary with respect to their cause. But still we may ask whether that which is necessary with respect to its cause has really any possibility by itself,' ואמנם רצה בן סיני שיסבים בואת החלוקה [בנליון : ממחוייב ואפשר למה שיש לו עלה ולמה שאין לו עלה] אל דעת הפילוסופים בנמצאות; וזה שהנרם השמימיי אצל כל הפילוסופים הוא הכרחי בזולתו. ואמנם האם הוא הכרחי בזולתו יש בו אפשרות בצרוף אל עצמו ,בו עיץ . ולזה היתה זאת הדרך מעוקשת כשילכו בה זה המחלך. Likewise in *Moreh ha-Moreh*, II, Prop. 12.

sophers in the use of the terms possibility and necessity.[46] Possibility, to Averroes, has only one meaning, and that is the real and primary one. Nothing whose existence is dependent upon external causes can, he holds, be called possible in any sense whatsoever. Avicenna's designation of sublunar and celestial elements as possible is, therefore, untenable; and his consequent proof for a self-existent cause is likewise invalid. The indivisibility of the divine essence as well as the unity of God does not follow indirectly from the proof of His necessary existence, but from the arguments, of which there are several, which directly prove His simplicity and unity.[47] And so, while disagreeing with Avicenna as to the proof, Averroes agrees with him that the divine attributes must be interpreted (1) as negatives, and (2) as external relations, the latter of which include

---

[46] Cf. *Destruction of the Destruction*, Disputation X. 'It has already been made clear from our arguments that if by necessary existence is understood that which has no cause, and by possible existence that which has a cause [i. e. the Avicennean view], the division of being into these two classes [i. e. necessary and possible] could not be asserted, for the opponent might deny this alleged division, maintaining that every existent being is without a cause. But if by absolute existence is meant necessary existence, and by possible is understood real possibility [i. e. the Averroean view], the series must undoubtedly terminate at an existence which has no cause.'

כבר קדם ממאמרנו שכאשר יובן מחוייב המציאות מה שאין עלה לו, ויובן מאפשר המציאות מה שיש עלה לו, לא תהיה חלוקת הנמצא בשני אלה הפרקים ידוע בה, כאשר לבעל דין לחלוק שאינו כמו שזכר, אבל כל נמצא אין עלה לו; אבן כאשר יובן ממחוייב המציאות הנמצא ההכרחי ומן האפשר, האפשר האמתי יכלה הענין בלא ספק אל נמצא אין עלה לו.

[47] Cf. Averroes' *Destruction of the Destruction*, Disputation VI. 'I say that this is a refutation of him who, like Avicenna, argues for the rejection of attributes from the premise of necessary existence by itself. But the best method to be followed in this inquiry is to argue from unity.' אמרתי זה כלו סתירה למי שהלך בהרחקת התארים דרך בן סיני, בהעמיד מחוייב המציאות בעצמותו; ואמנם הדרך היותר טובה בזה בחיוב ההתאחדות.

both the category of relation and that of action.[48] But these are not the only explanation of attributes. By a new theory of universals, which will presently be set forth, Averroes maintains that some attributes may be positive and essential.

Avicenna, as we have seen, holds the universals to have reality *in re* and *post rem* because of their reality *ante rem* in the mind of God. The pre-existent universals, according to him, are present in the multitudinous individuals. What then does Avicenna mean by his assertion that universals exist only in mind? He means by that that the presence of those universals in the individuals and our abstraction of them cannot be *discovered* except by the mind, though their presence in the individuals is independent of the mind. Averroes differs with him on that point. He thinks the very presence of the universals in the individuals a mere mental invention. The phrase that universals are in the mind he interprets to mean that the very presence of the universals in the individuals and their distinction therefrom is *invented* by the mind. The difference between Avicenna and Averroes is similar to the difference between the objective and subjective interpretations of Spinoza's definition of attribute in modern philosophy. Consequently in any definition the distinction between the individual substance which is defined and the universal substance by which it is defined has no reality whatsoever. The individual substance only appears to the mind in universal aspects. It is exactly this mentally invented distinction, says Averroes, that Aristotle conceives to exist between the faculties of the soul and its essence, and that also the Christian theologians conceive to exist between the three

[48] Cf. *Destruction of the Destruction*, Disputation V.

Personalities and the Godhead, though both the soul-essence and the Godhead are in reality one and absolutely indivisible.[49]

By this Averroes could have solved the entire problem of attributes. He could have said that the predicates attributed to God all designate certain aspects in which the divine essence appears to the human mind. He does not,

[49] Cf. *ibid*. 'It is in the nature of essential attributes that they do not actually diversify their subject; they diversify it only in the same sense as the parts of a definition are said to diversify the object defined, that is, what is called by the philosophers a mental plurality in contradistinction to an actual plurality. Take, for instance, the definition of man as a rational animal, in which case neither of these attributes nor both of them are actually added to the individual human essence, though man is diversified by the attributes describing appearance and form. Hence, it will follow that he who admits that the existence of the soul is absolutely independent of matter, will also have to admit that among immaterial existences there are such that are one in actuality though many in definition [that is to say, the soul is one in essence but many in faculties]. This is also the Christian doctrine of the Trinity, that is, they do not believe in attributes adjoined to the essence, for the attributes to them are only in definition, the manifoldness of which are not in actuality but in potentiality. Hence, they claim that these [personalities] are three and yet one, i. e. one in actuality but three in potentiality.' מדרך התארים העצמיים שלא יתרבה בם הנושא הסובל להם, אבל אמנם יתרבה בצד אשר יתרבה המוגדר בחלקי הגדר, וזה שהוא רבוי שכלי אצלם, לא רבוי בפועל, ר״ל, ודמיון זה, שהאדם אדם חי מדבר, ואין הדבור והחיות כל אחד מהם וכו׳ מחברו בו, ר״ל, בפועל. והמראה והתמונה מתרבה בו, ר״ל, ולזה יתחייב למי שיודה שהנפש אין מתנאי מציאותה החומר שיודה שכבר ימצא בנמצאות הנבדלות מה שהוא אחד בפועל, ר״ל, הרבה בגדר. וזהו דעת הנוצרים בשלוש, וזה, שהם לא יראים תארים נוספים על העצם, ואמנם הם אצלם מתרבים בגדר, והם רבים בכח ולא בפועל, ולזה יאמרו שהם שלשה ואחד, כלומר, אחד בפועל שלשה בכח.

This passage is paraphrased by Narboni in his commentary on the *Moreh* (I, 58), but he disagrees with Averroes as to the latter's interpretation of the Trinity. The Trinity according to the Christian belief, he says, are not potential but actual. והנראה לי כי התארים הנ׳ בפועל אצל הנוצרים והעצם אחד, לא שיהיה בכח כמו שיאמר ב״ר.

however, say so. He admits with Avicenna that all the attributes, which with regard to created beings are accidental, with regard to God must be interpreted either as negations or as dynamic and external relations.[50] There is one attribute, however, which he insists must be taken positively, and that is the attribute of Intelligence. Intelligence, says Averroes, is the essence of God. He maintains this to be the view of the Peripatetics in opposition to that of Plato.[51] Intelligence is therefore merely another word for God. In the proposition, 'God is intelligent', the relation affirmed between subject and predicate is not real but formal. And likewise the universality of that term, which is implied in its application to God and to human beings, is only nominal and formal.

Still, the nominalist interpretation of a universal term disposes only of the assumption of an underlying identity running through various individuals. But it has to assume the existence of some kind of relation and resemblance between different things. Without such an assumption the mind could not form universal terms at all. What is then the relation that must be assumed to exist between God and other creatures in order to justify the common application of the term Intelligence? The relation, according to Averroes, is that of cause and effect. God is a thinking being in whom the subject, object, and process of thinking are all one and the same thing. But His thinking is creative, and all the Intelligences as well as the human intelligence are offshoots of the divine intelligence. The application, therefore, of the term intelligence to God and to human beings does not mean that both share alike in

[50] Cf. *Destruction of the Destruction*, Disputation V.
[51] Cf. *ibid.*

a common property; it means than man derives his intelligence from God, in whom it is not a property but the very essence.

The universalization of an individual term by means of its application to the effects of that individual with which the term has originated is distinguished by Averroes as a class by itself. He designates such terms as ambiguous with respect to priority and posteriority of application. To get at the meaning of this phrase, we need enumerate all the other kinds of applicability of universal terms with which this new one is contrasted. Thus: single terms may be universally applied to different individuals in three ways—equivocally, univocally, and ambiguously.[52] A term is used equivocally when it is applied to two or more things which share nothing in common, either in essential or in non-essential properties. Such a term is a perfect homonym, and its several applications in reality are perfectly unrelated, as, to use an old example, the word *grammatica*, meaning the art of grammar and a woman. A univocal term is one which is applied to two things that share in an essential quality, as, for instance, the term 'man' applied to individual human beings. A term is ambiguous when it is applied to different individuals which share only in non-essential properties, e.g. '*white* snow' and '*white* paper'. We may recall that in Maimonides' theory the divine attributes are used neither univocally nor ambiguously, God sharing with other beings neither in essential nor in non-essential qualities. In that theory the attributes must be taken in

---

[52] Equivoca1 = משותפים or משתתפים; univocal = מוסכמים or מסכימים; ambiguous = מסופקים. Cf. Algazali's *Intentions*, I, *Logic*, I, 5 (כונות הגיון, אופן א׳ / חלוקה ה׳), and Maimonides' מלות ההגיון. Cf. Aristotle's Ὁμώνυμα, Συνώνυμα, Παρώνυμα, *Categories*, I.

an equivocal or homonymous sense. Divine intelligence, therefore, is absolutely unrelated with human intelligence, and is applied to God negatively. Now, Averroes proposes a new usage of a universal term in the case of its application to two things which share in a common quality only, in so far as one of them derives its quality from the other, to which it is essential. God, therefore, does not participate with man in intelligence, but God being intelligence, man derives his intelligence from Him. That special sense, in which a term may be applied to different things, was according to Averroes' testimony unknown to Avicenna.[53]

[53] Cf. Averroes' *Destruction of the Destruction*, Disputation VII. 'Ait Averroes: Si intellexisti id, quod diximus antea eo, quod sunt hic aliquae, quae includuntur uno nomine, non inclusione rerum univocarum, nec inclusione rerum aequivocarum, sed inclusione rerum relatarum ad aliud, quae dicuntur secundum prius, et posterius, et qualis proprietas harum rerum ut deveniant ad primum in illo genere, quod est causa prima omnibus, quibus imponitur hoc nomen, ut est nomen calidi, quod dicitur de igne, et aliis rebus calidis, et sicut est nomen entis, quod dicitur de substantia, et aliis accidentibus, et sicut nomen motus, quod dicitur de locali, et aliis motibus, non deficies scire inane, quod ingreditur in hoc sermone, nam nomen intellectus dicitur de intellectibus separatis apud philosophos secundum prius et posterius, quorum est intellectus primus, qui est causa aliorum, et sic est in substantia. Et ratio, quae demonstrat quod non habent naturam communem, est quoniam aliquis eorum est causa alterius, et id, quod est causa rei, est prius causati, et impossibile est ut sit natura causae, et causati uno genere, nisi in causis individualibus, et haec quidem species communicationis est contradicens communicationi genericae vero, quoniam communia genere, non est in eis primum, quod est causa aliorum, sed omnia sunt in gradu, et non reperitur in eis aliquid simplex, sed communia in re, quae dicuntur secundum prius, et posterius, necesse est ut sit in eis primum, et simplex, et hoc primum impossibile est ut imaginetur ei secundatio. Nam quotienscunque ponatur ei secundum, necesse est ut sit in gradu eius, quo ad esse, et naturam : et erit ibi natura communis eis, qua communicat communicatione generis veri ; et necesse est ut differant differentiis additis generi : ergo erit unumquodque ; eorum compositum ex genere, et differentia, et omne quod huiusmodi est innovatum. . Demum id, quod est in ultimitate perfectionis in esse, necesse est ut sit unum. Nam, nisi esset unum, im-

The new distinction in the universalization of terms which had been advanced by Averroes was adopted by Gersonides in his theory of divine attributes. Gersonides' constructive view may be gathered from his refutation of Maimonides. He commences by pointing out an inherent fallacy in the homonymous interpretation of positive attributes. Since all positive attributes that are not actions must be taken as homonyms, that is to say, affirming, according to the interpretation given above, a relation of perfect identity which emphasizes the negation of non-identity; and since consequently any predicate could thus be interpreted homonymously, what would account for the fact that some attributes are found in positive form whereas others occur only in negative form? Why should not the latter as well as the former be expressed in positive language? Take, for instance, the attributes of existence and incorporeality. If the former is perfectly homonymous, why should we not likewise affirm of God corporeality in an homonymous sense? To say that the sound of the word corporeality in itself, irrespective of its special meaning, is derogatory to the divine being, does not explain the matter. In dealing with the problem of attributes, we

_{possibile est ut sit ei ultimitas esse, id enim, quod est ultimitate non communicat ei aliud, nam, sicut linea una non habet ex uno latere duos fines, sic res, quae succedunt in esse, diversae quidem in additione, et diminutione, non habent duos fines ex uno latere. Avicenna autem nescivit in esse hanc naturam mediam inter naturam, quam significat nomen univocum et naturas, quae non communicant nisi nominibus tantum, aut accidenti remoto, et evenit ei haec dubitatio.' (Latin translation from the Hebrew of Averroes' *Hapalath ha-Hapalah*, in the tenth volume of Aristotle's collected works, p. 232 a–b, Venice, 1560.)}

It should be observed that this special kind of generic terms, which, according to Averroes, was unknown to Avicenna, is mentioned by Algazali in his *Intentions*, I; Logic, I, 5: נאותים ... והוא קיים בקדימה ואיחור, וכבר יקרא זה מסופק לחזרתו (כונות, הגיון, אופן א', חלוקה ח').

are chiefly concerned with the meaning of the terms as they are employed, and not with their associative connotations. Furthermore, the admissibility of attributes is decided upon the ground of their logical consonance with the conception of necessary existence, and not upon the consideration whether in human analogies they are regarded as perfections or imperfections. If the distinction of affirmative and negative prevails in the form of attributes, it follows that for quite different reasons the term existence, even when taken in a sense not entirely unrelated with its ordinary usage, may be affirmed of God, whereas the term corporeality under the same circumstances must not be affirmed of Him.[54]

---

[54] Cf. Gersonides' *Milḥamot*, III, 3. 'In general, if the things which we predicate of Him were applied to God and to ourselves in perfect homonymy, none of the terms which we use in designating ordinary things would be more appropriately used in reference to God as negation rather than affirmations or as affirmations rather than negations. Thus, for instance, one would be able to state that God is corporeal, provided he did not mean by that corporeality anything possessing quantity, but something which is perfectly homonymous with what we usually call corporeality. Likewise, one would be able to state that God is unknowing, if the term knowing in that proposition was not used to designate the same thing as that which we ordinarily call knowledge. Nor can it be maintained that we negate of God corporeality because with respect to ourselves it is an imperfection, but we affirm of Him knowledge because it is a perfection. For it is not the term corporeality, which is alone negated of God, that is an imperfection; the imperfection is rather contained in its meaning. That this is so can be proved by the fact that were we to designate by the term corporeality what is now designated by the term knowledge, and by the term knowledge what is now designated by the term corporeality, then corporeality would have been in respect to ourselves, perfection and knowledge would have been an imperfection. Furthermore, we do not affirm nor negate anything of God unless we had first ascertained as to whether the existence of that thing is appropriate of God or not, but it is not imperative upon us to inquire as to whether that thing is a perfection or an imperfection with respect to ourselves.'

Thus divine attributes are to be taken, according to Gersonides, as universal terms. But now the two objections raised by Maimonides recur. First, the attributes being universals, according to the accepted theory of universals, exist as parts in the objective individuals; this, however, is impossible in the case of God. Secondly, by attributing universals, you imply some kind of relation between God and created beings, and *ipso facto* you imply a similarity between them, and such a similarity is impossible.

Gersonides' answer to these two possible objections, as we have said, betrays the unmistakable influence of Averroes. He distinguishes between a real, or rather existential, universal and a nominal, the latter being found in the case where an individual quality of a cause, which is identical with the essence of that cause, is in common language applied to the effects of that cause. That term, with respect to the object with whose essence it is identical, is only an invented universal. When joined in a proposition, the relation between the subject and predicate is, therefore, not real but verbal. A subject of that kind, says Gersonides, may be called a 'subject of discourse', for in reality the subject and predicate are identical. It is only when the predicate is an accident that its relation with the subject is real, the latter being called a 'subject of existence', that is to say, the subject of inhesion of the accidental predicate. Now, in God all the attributes are identical with His essence, or, in other words, they have no separate existence whatsoever. In any proposition, therefore, in which we predicate some attributes of God we really state a relation of identity. Still, such statements are not tautological. For logical propositions do not merely express *real* relations, but *formal* relations also. God is the 'subject of discourse' of the attributes predicated of Him, and in discourse there is no tautology, for in discourse all the attributes predicated of God are universal terms. 'Knowledge', 'power', 'will', and all the other attributes, are affirmed of God and other beings in a related sense, the relation being that of cause and effect. But there is the following radical distinction between divine and human attributes. In God attributes are identical with His essence; in man they are accidental to it. In the technical language of the time this notion may be expressed as follows: The divine predicates are to be understood in a sense neither 'equivocal' nor 'univocal'; they are used in an 'ambiguous' sense with reference to the distinction of 'priority and posteriority'. To quote now Gersonides' own words:

'We say that after due reflection it appears that there are attributes that are applicable primarily to God and subsequently to other things besides Him without, however, implying plurality in God. For not every proposition in which something is affirmed of something implies plurality of that thing. There is implication of plurality only when one part of the proposition is the subject with respect to *existence* of the other part. But if it is not its subject with respect to existence, though it is its subject in the proposition, it does not follow that the subject is composite. For instance, if we state about a definite redness that it is a red colour, it does not follow that the redness is composed of colour and red, for colour is not the existent subject of red, but its subject of *discourse* only.'[55]

But would not a nominal universal which is derived from two individuals correlated as cause and effect, imply the existence of some real relation and similarity between the two individuals? Gersonides endeavours to show that it would not. If any relation is to be implied it will be

[55] Cf. *Milḥamot*, III, 3.

nominal, just as the universal itself is nominal. He cites an analogous case from the meaning of existence. Existence, according to Averroes, whose view is followed by Gersonides, is identical with the essence of the subject of which it is affirmed. Now, accidents exist through substances, the latter thus being the causes of the former. The term existence, therefore, is with respect to substances and accidents, a nominal universal implied to individuals which are causatively related. And yet there is no implication of the existence of any real relation between substance and accident. To quote Gersonides again:

'It can be shown, even though we admit that there can be no relation between God and His creatures, that the attributes predicated of God may be applied to Him primarily and to other beings subsequently. For there are some terms which, though they are applied to some things primarily and to others subsequently, do not imply a relation between those things. For instance, the term existence is applied to substance primarily and to accident subsequently as stated in the Metaphysics. Still it is clear that there is no relation between substance and accidents.'[56]

We turn now to the theory of divine attributes formulated by Moses Halavi.[57] Unlike Gersonides, Moses Halavi works out his theory independently of Maimonides, to whom he does not make the slightest allusion. His theory may be summarized as follows: Attributes are either positive or negative. Of the negative, some are so both in form (בשם) and in content (בעניין), as, for instance, 'incorporeality'. Others are negative only in content and positive in form, as, for instance, 'eternity', the real meaning of which is 'without beginning or end'. Both of these kinds of attri-

---

[56] Cf. *ibid*.　　[57] Cf. Steinschneider, *Uebersetzungen*, § 239.

butes are admissible. Thus far he is in perfect agreement with Maimonides.

Positive attributes are next divided by the author into three classes. First, attributes which are identical with the essence of the subject, as, for instance, animality in the predication of man. Second, attributes adjoined to the essence, as, for instance, whiteness, &c. Third, attributes which are merely descriptive of some external relation of the subject, as, for instance, actions and the relations of time and space. Of these three classes, the first and the last are admissible, but the second is inadmissible, for, adds the author, not only is any composition within the divine essence unthinkable, but likewise the composition of His essence with something outside itself.[58]

The points of difference between this theory and that of Maimonides are worth attention. First, according to Maimonides, actions and external relations are two different classes of attributes, the one admissible, the other inadmis-

[58] ואמנם התארים החיוביים, שם וענין, מהם תארים הם מהות המתואר, בתארנו אדם בשהוא חי: ומהם תארים אינם הם חלק מהות אלא יוצאים ממנו, ואבל הם יורו על תכונה במתואר מחוברת למהותו, בתארנו גד־ שהוא לבן; ומהם תוארים אינם מהות המתואר ולא הם תכונה מחוברת למהות, ואבל הם הלצות למתואר בצרוף אל דבר יצא ממנו, בתארנו גד בשהוא לימין דו, ואלה יקראו התוארים הצרופיים. אמנם התארים אשר הם חלק המהות אינם מיוחסים לו ית׳, אחר שכבר התבאר שעצמותו ית׳ בלתי מתחלקת. ואמנם התארים אשר הם במהות המתואר, הנה מן הידוע שתואר אותו ית׳ בהם אפשרי, אחר שלא יורו על ענין נוסף על המהות כלל ... ומפני שתארי ית׳ באלו התארים הצרופיים נכון, אנחנו מתארים אותו בסביית, ובהתחליית ... כי אלה כלם תארים צרופיים ... הנה התבאר שהוא ית׳ נכון לתארו בתארים השוללים, וזה אם במלות תנין, ואם בענין בלתי מלות, ושתארי החיובים אשר בעצמותו ואשר הם על דרך הצרוף עובר.

sible; according to Moses Halavi both fall under the heading of external relations and both are admissible.[59] Halavi, again, in contradistinction to Maimonides, calls essential universal attributes identical with the individual essence, and admits the usage in divine predications. This unmistakably proves that to him universals are merely mental inventions.

Reverting, then, to his first class of positive attributes, to those designating a universal essential quality, which he holds to be identical with the essence of the individual subject, like Gersonides, Moses Halavi endeavours to obviate the possible objection based on the proposition that identity cannot be a relation in a logical proposition. ' In answer to such an objection ', he says, ' we maintain that the predicate of a proposition, as, for example, " He is knowing ", with respect to its general meaning of the comprehension of external objects, is not identical with the subject. Nay, they are radically different terms, for the term " knowing " does not imply the specific subject of the proposition. It is with respect to this general meaning that the predicate bears a real and unidentical relation to the subject. Sometimes, however, it may be warranted by the context of the proposition, that the apprehension implied in the predicate with regard to the subject should be taken in a specific sense which is identical with the subject, as, for example, in the proposition, " God is knowing ". It is in accordance with this distinction between the two aspects of the predicate that we are enabled to attribute to God essential qualities which are distinct from Him as subject

[59] ומפני שתארי ית׳ באלו התארים הצרופיים נכון, אנחנו מתארים אותו בסבית, ובהתחליית, ובבריאה, ובעשייה, וזולת זה מה שדומה לו, כי אלה כלם תארים צרופיים, כי ענינם שמציאות זולתו נשפעת מטציאותו.

and predicate, but do not imply plurality in His essence.'[60]

The implication of this passage is clear. Essential attributes are universalized by the mind. They are mere aspects of the individual objects in which they have neither objective nor subjective existence. But it is that mentally invented universal aspect of the individual subject that is affirmed in a logical proposition. The relation between subject and predicate is, therefore, merely formal, and God, though identical with His attributes, can still be their formal subject in a proposition.

In these five theories of divine attributes, which we have analysed, the points of agreement and disagreement are clear. They all agree that Biblical predications of God should be taken as logical judgements. All but Algazali accept the Avicennean definition of the absolute simplicity of the divine essence, though they do so for different reasons. The controversy turns merely on the reality of the universal predicates and their distinction from the

[60] וכבר יקשה המקשה, הנה תאמר שכל גזרה יחוייב שנשואה ונושאה
יהיו משתנים עם היות אחד מהם נשא לאחר. ואמנם כשהיה נשואה
ונושאה דבר אחד בעינו, הנה אין שם נושא ונשוא באמת, אבל יהיה
מובן המאמר אשר בזה לא יגיע ממנו תועלת בין שהולץ מאותו הענין
בשם אחד כמו שאמרנו שהאדם אדם, או בשני שמות נרדפים, באמרנו
שהחטור עיר, כי זה [דומה] לאמרנו שהחמור חמור ... והתשובה על
זאת הקושיא, שנשוא זאת הגזרה, והוא אמרנו יודע בבחינה הוראתה על
ענין הידיעה משולח אינו נרדף לנושאה, אבל הם שני שמות נבדלים,
כי אמרנו יודע לו מובן בלתי מובן נושא הגזרה, ומזה הצד לוקח
אחד מהם נשוא והאחר נושא. אכן קרה לידיעה בצרוף אל זה העצמות
המתואר בה שהיו דבר אחד בעינו במציאות, וזה דבר יוצא ממובן הגזרה,
והוא אמרנו שהאל יודע, הנה על דרך הזה יתאמת שיתואר ית' בתארים
אשר הם עצמותו, ויתחייב מזה הנושא והנשוא, מבלתי שיתחייב הרכבה
בעצמות.

subject. And on this point, too, they all further agree that in God the universal cannot in any way be distinct from His individuality. The inquiry is, therefore, reduced to the following two questions: First, are the universal essential attributes in beings other than God distinct from their individual essence or not? Second, in what sense are these universals applied to God as predicates? The answer to the latter questions is dependent upon that given to the former. Maimonides, believing that in other beings the universals are distinct from the individual essences, is forced to interpret the divine predicates as homonymous, that is to say, as absolutely individual terms, entirely unrelated with other terms of the same sound. Averroes, however, believing that all essential universals are mere names, interprets the predicate of intelligence in its application to God as a universal term used ambiguously *secundum prius et posterius*. Gersonides and Halavi follow Averroes, but extend his interpretation of the predicate Intelligence to all other predicates. With this, we are ready for our discussion of Crescas.

(To be continued.)

REPRINTED FROM THE JEWISH QUARTERLY REVIEW
NEW SERIES
VOLUME VII, NUMBER 2

CRESCAS ON THE PROBLEM OF
DIVINE ATTRIBUTES (II-III)

BY
HARRY AUSTRYN WOLFSON

PHILADELPHIA, 1916
THE DROPSIE COLLEGE FOR HEBREW AND COGNATE LEARNING
1916

CRESCAS ON THE PROBLEM OF DIVINE ATTRIBUTES

By Harry Austryn Wolfson, Harvard University.

CHAPTER II
Crescas's Criticism of Maimonides.

POSITIVE attributes, contends Crescas, cannot be inadmissible, for that would reduce the accomplished metaphysician in his knowledge of the divine being to the same level with the novice. But that the knowledge of the divine is commensurate with one's moral and intellectual perfections is generally admitted.[61] True, Maimonides had forestalled that objection by declaring that though there can be no rising scale in the positive knowledge of God there can still be one in the discovery of additional negations. His explanation, however, is inadequate, for the augmentation of negative attributes cannot mark an increase in knowledge. True knowledge must be scientific and demonstrative, a principle which had been advanced by Aristotle[62] and upheld by Maimonides.[63] It is not the acquisition of new facts, but rather the invention of new proofs that knowledge grows by. Now, that positive attributes are to be rejected is demonstrable by a simple argument based upon the proposition of divine absolute existence—an argument which can be easily mastered even

[61] Cf. *Moreh*, I. 59.   [62] Cf. *Physics*, I, 1.
[63] Cf. *Moreh*, I, 55.

by those uninitiated in philosophy. And once one has mastered demonstration of the divine absolute existence one can prove the inadmissibility of any positive attribute that may come up. Any additional negation merely involves a new application of the identical argument, and thus adds nothing to the content of knowledge. Hence Crescas asks with added emphasis: Since the divine essence is unknowable, and if you also deny the existence of essential attributes, how can there be a rising scale in the knowledge of the divine being?[64]

Again, the inadmissibility of divine attributes is irreconcilable with tradition. If the divine qualities are all identical with the divine essence, then in the prayer of Moses, to be shown God's glory,[65] what the prophet had asked for was to attain the knowledge of God's essence. But it is highly improbable that Moses should have been ignorant of the fact that the divine essence was unknowable. Furthermore, tradition has differentiated the Ineffable Name from other divine names in that the former refers to the divine nature itself, whereas the latter are derivative of His actions. Now, since the divine essence is unknowable the Ineffable Name could not have been a designation thereof. And if you also say that no essential attributes are existent, then it could not as well designate any divine attribute. What part of the divine nature could it then have referred to? You could not say that it designated God's absolute existence or some of His negative attributes, for if that were the case, the meaning of the Ineffable Name would not have been kept in secrecy. Hence, positive attributes are not inadmissible.[66]

[64] Cf. *Or Adonai*, I, III, 3, p. 23 a.   [65] Cf. Exodus 33. 18.
[66] Cf. *Or Adonai*, I, III, 3, p. 23 b.

Nor are relative attributes inadmissible. If you say that predications expressing temporal, spatial, or some other external relations of God, though not implying a plurality in His essence, are inadmissible because all such relations, if real, imply similarity, why then is the affirmation of actions admissible? Actions, to be sure, when conceived as emanative from the divine essence, co-existing *with* Him always in energy and never *within* Him as a mere capacity, do not by themselves imply the inherence of external, imperfect qualities. On that account, Maimonides is perfectly consistent in rejecting positive attributes and admitting actions. But still actions are external relations. However they are taken, actions express some relation between God and the external, created reality, a relation which, like transient qualities, is changeable and transitional, even though unlike the latter it does not imply changeability and transitionality in the essences of the related objects. For even though we may explain the apparent changeability in the divine actions as due to the material objects operated upon rather than to the operative agent, those actions, when not viewed as dynamic forces, but as external static relations between the agent and its object, must of necessity like all external relations, and especially like the relation between transient agents and their objects, be changeable and transitional. That actions present a phase of external relativity is an indisputable assumption. In fact, as we have already pointed out, Maimonides stands alone in differentiating between actions and external relations and separating them into two distinct classes of predicables. Most of the philosophers had included actions in the class of external relations, permitting the use of the latter as well as that of the former. And so, since Maimonides prohibits external relations on account of similarity, why should he not for the same reason prohibit actions?[67]

In his discussion of external relations, Maimonides especially mentions the two classes enumerated by Aristotle;[68] first, the relation of reciprocity, and, second, the rotation of degree of comparison. The former is designated by him by the term הצטרפות, Arabic اضافة, and the latter by the term יחס, Arabic نسبة. Both of these kinds are inadmissible. In rejecting the former kind, he states its reason that it is characteristic of such correlatives to be reciprocally convertible. The contention of this phrase has been variously interpreted by the commentators, and, as usual,

---

[67] Cf. *Or Adonai*, I, III, 3, p. 23 a. 'Since attributes by which a thing is described in its relation to something else, which implies non-existence, are inadmissible with respect to God, as e. g. the transition of an object from a state of potentiality to that of actuality [*Moreh*, II, 55], how then does he allow the use of attributes which only describe the actions of an object, as e. g. doing, acting, creating; since these, too, imply non-existence; for before the deed, act or creation, the agent was potential and afterwards became actual.'

The meaning of this argument had been misunderstood by Abraham Shalom and Isaac Abrabanel. They interpreted the argument as follows: Since essential attributes are to be rejected on account of the implication of transition from potentiality to actuality, why should not actions be rejected for the same reason. And so both of them point out Crescas's error in overlooking the distinction drawn by Maimonides himself between essential attributes and actions. (Cf. נוה שלום, מ' י״ב, דרוש א', פ״ב.)

הנה התבאר ממה שאמר הרב שאין תוארי הפעולות לומר פעל ועשה יורה שהיה בכח ושב בפועל, כמו שאמר זה החכם. ויש להפליא ממנו איך אמר זה אחרי ראותו לשון הרב פ' י״ח הנזכר.

Cf. also Abrabanel's commentary on the *Moreh*, I, 55. The rendering of this argument by Dr. Julius Wolfsohn (*Der Einfluss Gazali's auf Chisdai Crescas*, p. 38, note 2) is uncritical. Cf. also Kaufmann, *Attributenlehre*, p. 416, note 85.

[68] Cf. *Organon, Categories*, ch. 7.

the ancients like Profiat Duran, Asher Crescas, Shem-tob, and Abrabanel had come nearer the truth than the moderns, like Solomon Maimon, Munk, and Friedländer. From the *Organon*[69] we may gather the meaning of the statement to be as follows. Correlations are reciprocal not because of a reciprocal relation existing between two objects in reality, but because terms by which the related objects are designated are mutually implicative. Thus, 'slave' and 'master' are reciprocally correlative, but 'John' and 'master' are not so, though in reality John may be the slave of the master. Likewise, 'wing' and 'winged creature' are reciprocally correlative, but 'wing' and 'bird' are not, though the bird is a winged creature. Suppose now that the term 'slave' were used homonymously, in a sense absolutely divorced from its original meaning, would it still be correlative with 'master'? In other words, must a reciprocal correlation be so in reality as well as in name? Maimonides seems to think that the two conditions are necessary. Reciprocally correlative terms must be mutually implicative in name and mutually interdependent in reality. Consequently he maintains that by whatever term you designate God, that term taken as it must be in an absolute sense is perforce a homonym, and therefore no reciprocal relation can exist between God and other beings. Thus, even if God is called the First Cause or Principle, unlike all other causes and principles, it is absolutely independent of its effect and consequence. 'For', says Maimonides, 'it is characteristic of two correlatives by reciprocation to be mutually convertible, and God being necessary existence and everything besides being possible existence, there can be no such correlation between them.' But, argues Crescas,

[69] Cf. *ibid.*

while it is true that the divine existence, viewed as mere existence, is absolute and independent of anything else, when however it is viewed as causative existence it is because that in its causative nature it is even in reality dependent upon the existence of effects emanating from its essence. His existence is necessary because it is not anteceded by any prior cause, but it is causative because it is creative. The fact that His causativity is dependent upon the existence of its effects does not detract from the necessity of His own existence. For necessary existence means nothing but the absence of efficient causation. And thus while the divine existence is absolute, the divine causation is not.[70]

Furthermore, if time be eternal, God would share with it in the common property of eternity. To understand the full significance of this criticism we must first cite Aristotle's

[70] Cf. *Or Adonai*, I, III, 3, p. 23 b. 'It is difficult to comprehend the statement made by Maimonides, namely, that there can be no perfect relation between God and His creatures on account of the condition that objects which are correlative must be reciprocally convertible. For, as a matter of fact, God must inevitably be conceived as Cause and Principle. Since a cause is so with respect to its effects and a principle likewise with respect to what follows from it, it is therefore evident that in this respect there exists some relation between them.'

I take this argument of Crescas to be an application of Algazali's contention that necessary existence only implies the negation of prior causes. Algazali's contention, as will be seen, reappears again in Crescas's exposition of his own theory of Attributes (cf. *infra*, ch. III, note 110). In this argument, therefore, Crescas is reasoning from his own premise. It is, truly speaking, not an argument against Maimonides. Of the same nature, as will be pointed out, is Crescas's next argument from time.

This underlying postulate of Crescas's argument seems to have been overlooked by Abraham Shalom (cf. נוה שלום מ' י״ב ד״א פ' נ׳) and Abrabanel (cf. פירוש המורה ח״א פ' נ״ב), cf. also Kaufmann, *Attributenlehre*, p. 389, note 47, and Julius Wolfsohn, *Der Einfluss Gazali's auf Chisdai Crescas*, p. 38, note 1.

definition of the phrase 'being in time'. To be in time may mean two things, one, to co-exist *with* time, and, the other, to exist *in* time and be measured by it.[71] The second meaning, however, is rejected by Aristotle as being untrue. When, therefore, Maimonides queries whether there be any relation between God and time, he simply means whether it could be affirmed that God has existence *in* time, to which his answer is in the negative, for since time is consequent to motion, and motion to magnitude,[72] an inextended being cannot be said to have temporal existence in that sense. But the question is now raised by Crescas: Why cannot temporal relation be affirmed of God in the sense of co-existence *with* time, or to be when time is? The relation would then not be, as in the first case, of the dependence of God upon time, but rather of the commonality of eternal co-existence of two independent entities, God and time. The hypothesis of eternal time, to be sure, is rejected by Maimonides, but that is on quite other grounds, and not because time, were it eternal, could not share with God the property of eternity.[73]

Maimonides' rejection of temporal relation in the case of God is still less justifiable 'in view of what has been said in the second part in refutation of the premise that time is an accident consequent to motion'.[74] Herein Crescas is pitting his own definition of time with all its corollaries against that of Maimonides, rather than criticizing the latter

[71] Cf. *Physics*, IV, 12, § 8.   [72] Cf. *ibid.*, IV, 12, § 6.

[73] Cf. *Or Adonai*, I, III, 3, p. 23 b. 'Likewise with regard to his statement that there is no relation between God and time, even if we admit that time is one of the conditions of motion, the latter of which is a condition of corporeal objects, there can still be a relation and similarity between God and time with respect to eternity, especially if we assume that time is eternal.'   [74] Cf. *ibid.*

from his own premises. Following Aristotle, Maimonides defines time as an accident adjoined to motion, and to be in time is circumscribed by two conditions. In the first place, the temporal object must have motion,[75] and in the second place, it must be comprehended by the time,[76] thus not co-existing with the whole of the time, but only with a part thereof. Therefore, the eternal translunary spheres, according to Aristotle, which are endowed with rotary motion, thus satisfying only one of the conditions, are said to be in time only by accident. The eternal immovable Intelligences, however, satisfying neither of the conditions, are not in time at all. And so God has no temporal relation. Though God is said to have existed prior to the world, the priority referred to is causal rather than temporal, since prior to the emergence of matter there had been no time. But Crescas defines time as an accident of both motion and rest, meaning by the latter some positive entity and not a mere absence of motion.[77] Time, therefore, being independent of motion, is likewise independent of matter, and had existed even before the creation of the universe. And so, the immovable eternal beings as well as God may be said to have existence in time.

Finally,[78] the divine negative attributes cannot form a privative judgement; they must of necessity form a negative judgement, thus involving an indirect affirmation. Privative judgements are possible only in the case where the subject belongs to a different universe of discourse from that which the predicate belongs to. When we say that 'a mathematical point is not red', the judgement must truly be

---

[75] Cf. *Physics*, IV, 12, § 11. [76] Cf. *ibid.*, IV, 12, § 10.
[77] *Or Adonai*, I, I, XVI, p. 11 a, and I, II, XI, p. 19 a.
[78] *Ibid.*, I, III, III, p. 25 a.

privative, denying red as well as all its correlatives, 'not red' thus meaning colourless, because in the universe of mathematical points there is no colour. But in the proposition 'God is not ignorant', while we negate not only human ignorance but also human knowledge, still, according to Maimonides, we affirm of God some knowledge which is identical with the divine essence, and which has no known relation with human knowledge. Thus the negation of knowledge in the case of God cannot be an absolute privation of knowledge; it must only be a negation of human knowledge which indirectly implies the affirmation of divine knowledge. Since divine knowledge is thus affirmed by the negation of human knowledge, the two must have some kind of relation, however vague and inarticulate. Divine knowledge, says Crescas, must accordingly be 'some kind of apprehension'. Now, let us designate that 'some kind of apprehension' by the letter X, and see whereabouts it would lead us.[79]

[79] Cf. *Or Adonai*, I, III, 3, p. 25 a. 'It is quite evident that when we attribute to God knowledge and power in a particular sense, meaning by knowledge the negation of its counterpart, namely, *human knowledge* [literally, ignorance], and by power, the negation of *human power* [literally, impotence], either of these two terms ascribed to Him must of necessity imply something positive. For even though His knowledge is as different from our knowledge as His essence differs from our essence, still that which is implied in the negation of *human knowledge* [literally, ignorance] must be some kind of comprehension or perception. That the negation of *human knowledge* [literally, ignorance] must imply [the affirmation of] something positive and cognoscible, is beyond dispute, since [being] the counterpart of that [negated] *human knowledge* [literally, ignorance], [it] must indicate a certain [positive] thing, namely, some kind of perception.'

I have translated the term סותר by 'counterpart' rather than by 'contrary', throughout these passages. I have likewise taken the terms סכלות and לאות to mean respectively human knowledge and human ignorance in general, which in contrast with divine knowledge and power,

First, what would be the relation of that X to the divine essence? It cannot be accidental nor essential to it, since both are debarred by Maimonides. It must, therefore, be identical with the essence. But X, as we have said, is not entirely unknowable; for so much is known of it that it is 'some kind of apprehension'. The question is now, Is it co-extensive with the essence or not? In the former case, the essence would have to be knowable; and in the latter, the essence would have to be composed of a knowable and unknowable part.[80]

Furthermore, as X stands for the divine correlative of human knowledge, so would Y stand for the divine correlative of human power. Now, since human knowledge and power are different, X and Y will have to be different.

are nothing but ignorance and impotence at their best. For I think that Crescas understood the term 'negative attributes', used by Maimonides, in the same sense as I interpreted it in ch. I. According to my rendering and interpretation of this argument as well as of those that follow, the objections raised against them by Abraham Shalom in his *Neveh Shalom* are ill-founded. (Cf. *Neveh Shalom*, XII, I, IV; Jöel, *Don Chasdai Crescas*, p. 31; cf. also *Eș Ḥayyim* by Aaron ben Elijah the Karaite, ch. 71.)

[80] Cf. *Or Adonai*, I, III, 3, p. 25 a. 'Therefore I say that if this comprehension and whatever it implies were not something positive and essential to the Blessed One, it would have to be His essence itself, inasmuch as it could not be an accidental attribute, since God can bear no relation whatsoever to accidents. Now, if it were His essence itself, it would give rise to either of these two absurdities. First, were His essence to include nothing but what we understand by the term comprehension, His essence would then have to be knowable. Second, were His essence to include something besides what we understand by the term comprehension, it would then have to be composed of two parts, namely, that which we understand by the term comprehension and that of which we have no knowledge at all. Either of these two consequences is absolutely absurd. That the divine essence cannot be an object of our knowledge, is well known to every novice in Metaphysics; and that His essence cannot likewise be composed of two parts is due to the fact that God would in that case have one possible existence.' (Cf. *Neveh Shalom*, *ibid.*)

Hence, if these attributes were identical with God's essence, His essence would be composite.

Finally, suppose, however, that X is absolutely unrelated with human knowledge, and that is not even 'some kind of apprehension'. The proposition 'God is knowing', which according to Maimonides means that 'God is not ignorant', would, therefore, be the exclusion of human knowledge and the lack thereof without at the same time affirming divine knowledge.[81] But the judgement could not be privative, for though the divine knowledge is absolutely unrelated to the human knowledge, and cannot therefore be indirectly affirmed by the negation of the latter, there is, however, an absolutely unique divine knowledge which cannot be denied in the same way as we can deny mathematical colour. And so, negative attributes form negative judgements. But according to Maimonides negative attributes mean that God neither possesses those attributes as they are stated, nor their opposites. This, however, is contrary to the law of excluded middle.[82]

[81] Cf. *ibid.* 'Again, it has been shown, that the terms knowledge and power, when applied to God, must mean something positive and cognoscible, since in the case of negating [of God] either *human knowledge* [literally, ignorance] or *human power* [literally, impotence] we must understand [indirectly to affirm of Him] something [positive], namely, either the [divine] counterpart of *human knowledge* [literally, ignorance] or the [divine] counterpart of *human power* [literally, impotence]. But it is clear that whatever is meant by the [divine] counterpart of *human knowledge* [literally, ignorance] is not identical with whatever is meant by the [divine] counterpart of *human power* [literally, impotence]. Consequently the meaning of the one must differ from that of the other. Hence it follows that neither of them can be taken as identical with the divine essence, for in that case His essence would be composed of different parts.' (Cf. *Neveh Shalom, ibid.*)

[82] Cf. *ibid.* 'Again, if his conclusion with regard to the denial of essential attributes were true . . . . . it would be impossible to affirm of God any positive implication of those attributes, inasmuch as the denial thereof is not because we are ignorant of any of His essential attributes but because

From his arguments against Maimonides' theory of attributes, Crescas passes over to a discussion of the relation between essence and existence. In its origin, among the Arabs and Jews, the problem of essence and existence was much simpler than in its later development among the Schoolmen. To the latter the problem presented itself in the following form. Assuming the presence of a distinction between essence and existence within actual beings they ask, What does that distinction consist in?[83] The various answers given to the question ran parallel to the solutions offered to the problem of universals, real, conceptual, or nominal. This evolved form of the problem, however, bears only a remote resemblance to what seems to have been its nucleus, namely, the controversy of Avicenna and Averroes. To these Arabic thinkers the problem of essence and existence presented itself in the form whether existence is an accidental or an essential universal, and it originated in the following manner:

That which is divided into the ten Categories is designated by Aristotle by the word τὸ ὄν. The corresponding Arabic term is الموجود, a passive participle from a root meaning 'to find' (وجد). In the Arabic language that

---

He does not possess any. Thus, God will have to be deprived of whatever we understand by comprehension or power. Neither of these can, therefore, be ascribed to Him either as parts of His essence or as essential attributes. But as it is evident that any kind of ignorance or impotence [i. e. human knowledge and power] must be negated of Him, it follows that He is negated both contraries or opposites, namely, knowledge [i. e. divine] and ignorance [i. e. human knowledge], power [i. e. divine], and impotence [i. e. human power].' But that is most absurd and inane (cf. *Neveh Shalom*, ibid. ; Joël, *Don Chasdai Crescas*, p. 31 ; Kaufmann, *Attributenlehre*, p. 478, note 162 ; Julius Wolfsohn, *Einfluss Algazalis*, p. 40).

[83] Cf. R. P. Kleutgen, *La Philosophie scholastique*, vol. III, chap. II; M. De Wulf, *Scholasticism Old and New*, pp. 108-9.

passive participle joined to a noun A in the nominative case forms a proposition meaning 'A is existent'. Now, in this proposition, it is clear, that the existence affirmed of A must be accidental to it, for were it identical with the essence of A, argues Avicenna, 'A is existent' would mean 'A is A'. Existence is thus an accident. 'Being', τὸ ὄν, or الموجود, which is divided into the ten categories, is therefore resolvable into 'that which is', having itself existence superadded to its essence, and so is existence accidental to the essence of all the ten categories. And, like all accidents, existence is applied to different subjects in unequal sense. Meaning independent reality outside the mind, existence is primarily applied to substances which are self-existent, and through these to the accidents of quality and quantity, and through qualitatively or quantitatively modified substances, it is also applied to the residual accidents.[84] As the com-

[84] According to Isaac Albalag (commentary on Algazali's *Intentions*) the problem of essence and existence and unity had its origin in two apparently contradictory statements which he alleges to be found in the works of Aristotle. In the Metaphysics (IV, 2) Aristotle identifies being (τὸ ὄν) and unity (τὸ ἕν) with the essence of the subject of which they are predicated. In *De Anima*, however, says Albalag, being and unity are stated to be accidental to essence.

ואבוחמד טעה בזה, לפי שלקח המצוי הנאמר על ענין הראשון, והוא אשר אליו כיון אריסטו בספר הנפש תחת המצוי הנאמר על ענין השני, והוא אשר כיון במה שאחר הטבע (יצחק אלבלג, פירוש על הכוונות, אלהיות, ט״א).

I was, however, unable to identify Albalag's reference in *De Anima*. In *De Anima*, II, 1, 7, the only place in that book where being and unity are discussed, there is no indication that Aristotle had considered them as accidents.

Cf. also Shemtob's commentary on the *Moreh*, I, 57.

In my exposition of the reason that had led Avicenna to consider existence as an accident, I have followed Averroes. (Cf. *Destruction of the Destruction*, Disputation VII ; *Epitome of the Metaphysics*, I. The latter passage is quoted by Munk, *Guide*, vol. I, ch. 57, p. 231. Paraphrases of

position of essence and existence, which is now assumed in every being, must necessarily be occasioned by a preceding cause, that cause itself, in order to avoid an infinite

this passage of Averroes is found in almost every commentary on the *Moreh*; cf. also *infra*, note 86).

The following observation on the meaning of the Hebrew words ישות, מציאות, מהות, may be of some interest. In early Hebrew translations from the Arabic the terms ישות (being) and מציאות (existence), were synonymous, both contrasted with מהות (quiddity), cf. Hebrew translation of Algazali's *Intentions*, Part II, Metaphysics.

וזה יראה מה שזכרנוהו קודם מפני הישות אשר הוא מליצה מהמציאות בלתי המהות.

In the Hebrew translation of Aegidius de Colonna's *De Esse et Essentia*, however, the term מציאות is used as synonymous with מהות, both of which are contrasted with ישות.

א״כ מבואר הוא שהישות הוא דבר אחר מהמציאות או המהות לבד (p. 96).

The following explanation seems to me to be quite plausible.

The Arabs, and after them the Jews, rendered the Greek οὐσία and τὸ ὄν, both from a root meaning 'to be', by وجود (מציאות) and موجود (נמצא), which, derived from the root 'to find', usually mean 'existence' and 'existent', respectively. In addition to 'existence', they coined the term ماهيّة (מהות), that is, 'quiddity'. 'Existence' was to them the accident of 'quiddity'. And so even when οὐσία and τὸ ὄν are translated literally by (הוה) كاين and كون (ישות or חיות), from 'to be', the latter are considered as synonymous with 'existence' and therefore accidents of 'quiddity'. According to Averroes, as we shall see, the distinction of 'existence' and 'quiddity' originally sprang from that inaccurate Arabic translation of the term οὐσία.

Now, the Scholastics used the term *essentia* among other terms for the Greek οὐσία. Adopting from the Arabs the *quidditas* they used it synonymously with *essentia*. Again, the Arabic وجود (מציאות) became *esse* which, as is well known, is used by the Schoolmen in the sense of *existentia*. Likewise, the Arabic موجود (נמצא) became *ens*. And just as the Arabs and Jews used to speak of the distinction between 'existence' and 'quiddity' so they speak of the distinction between *esse* and *essentia seu quidditas* or *ens* and *essentia seu quidditas*.

Thus while the Hebrew מציאות and the Latin *essentia* are both originally translations from the Greek οὐσία, in the historical development of ideas

chain of cause and effect, we must assume to be free from that composition. Thus Avicenna concludes that in God there is no distinction of essence and existence.[85]

they have drifted away far apart from each other. *Essentia* is identical with מהות, which is quite the opposite of מציאות, and מציאות is identical with *esse*, which is the antithesis of *essentia*.

Some of the Hebrew translators from the Latin saw that point clearly. Thus the translator of Thomas Aquinas renders the title of the latter's *De ente et essentia* by מאמר בנמצא ובמהות (quoted by Steinschneider, *Uebersetzungen*, § 295, 5). He likewise translates literally *essentia* by היות and *ens* by הוה, giving, however, for the latter its traditional Hebrew equivalent נמצא.

שאלה א׳, אם שם ההיות, ובלשונם אישינסיא, הוא לקוח משם ההוה,
ר"ל, הנמצא, ובלשונם איניש, במהות ובמציאות מטומש (quoted *ibid.*).

The translator of Aegidius, however, renders the title *De esse et essentia* by מאמר הנמצא והמציאות. This, as we have seen, is inaccurate. For *ens* is נמצא, and *esse* is מציאות. Again, while both *essentia* and מציאות are translations from the Greek οὐσία, their meanings are quite different. He likewise renders the phrase *essentia seu quidditas* by המציאות או המהות, the first part of which is wrong again for the same reason. It should be observed that the phrase *seu quidditas*, which the translator had in his Latin text, is not found in the Venice edition of 1503 of Aegidius's *De esse et essentia*.

[85] There is a very important question which I wish to raise at this point. In the literature dealing with the problem of essence and existence we find two different formulas which are invariably used in affirming the absence of any distinction between essence and existence in the divine being.

The first formula employed by Maimonides and some of his commentators states that in God *essence and existence are identical*. The following quotations will illustrate it:

תהיה מציאותו עצמו ואמתתו, ועצמו מציאותו (מורה, ח"א, פ׳, נ"ז)
אחר שהש"י הוא מחוייב המציאות, ומציאותו ומהותו דבר אחד (שם טוב, פרוש על המורה שם).

לפי שמציאותו ומהותו אחד ... אבל מציאותו הוא מהותו (אפודי, שם, פ׳ נ"ח).

הנה הם מסכימים על הנמצא הנאמר על האלוה ית׳ שאינו דבר יוצא מעצמו (אור ה׳, מ"א, כ"ג, פ"א).

In opposition to this view, Averroes maintains that existence is identical with essence. The two are indistinguishable even in thought. Anything thought of is thought

The second formula used by Avicenna and Algazali states that God is *existence without essence added to it*. To illustrate:

ולכן היתה העלה הראשונה מציאות בלי מהות נוספת (אלמלי, כוות אלהיות, מ"א).

בבטול אמרם שהראשון הוא נמצא משום בלי מהות (הנ"ל, הפלת הפילוסופים, שאלה ח').

The question may now be raised whether these two different formulas are advisedly used, implying two distinct theories, or not. For several reasons it would seem that the two formulas do not imply two different theories. First, as far as we know, there is no record of any controversy between Maimonides and Avicenna and Algazali as to whether in God essence and existence are identical or He is existence without essence. Maimonides is generally believed to follow Avicenna and Algazali on that point, even though they use different formulas. Second, from the following quotations it may be conclusively deduced that the two formulas are used indiscriminately.

והש"י אמרו בו שהוא מציאות ולא מהות, לפי שהישות והמהות הוא אחד בו (קרשקש, פירוש על המורה ח"א, פ', נ"ז).

ואינו מחוייב מזה שנשיג ישותו המיוחדת אשר הוא מהותו, שהוא מציאות בלי מהות נוסף, וכמו שאמר אבוחמ"ד אין מציאות בלי מהות כי אם לאל (הנ"ל, שם, פ' נ"ח).

But the following passage from Isaac Albalag's commentary on Algazali's *Intentions of the Philosophers*, would on the other hand indicate quite clearly that Albalag had taken the latter's formula that God is *existence without essence* quite literally.

לפיכך אמר שהעילה הראשונה מציאות בלא מהות, וזה תימה גדול איך שלל לעילה הראשונה המהות שאינו דבר נוסף על העצם וחייב לי המציאות שהוא מקרה (אלבלג, כוות אלהיות, מ"א).

Again, from the following passage in Averroes' *Destruction of the Destruction*, Disputation VIII, it would also seem that this was a point at issue between Algazali and Averroes as to the interpretation of Avicenna's theory, the former maintaining that it meant that God is *existence without essence*, the latter that in God *essence and existence are identical*.

אמר ב"ר ... זה הפרק כלו מטעה, כי האנשים לא יניחו לראשון

of as existent. This essential existence, to be sure, cannot be affirmed as the predicate of a subject in a logical proposition without involving tautology. But conceptual existences may have counterparts in reality, or may not have them. The idea of God and angels, for instance, has something in reality to correspond with it. The idea of centaurs on the other hand, though likewise involving existence, has nothing outside the mind to correspond with it. The former idea is, therefore, a true one ($\dot{\alpha}\lambda\eta\theta\acute{\eta}s$—صادق—צודק), the latter idea is a false one ($\psi\epsilon\upsilon\delta\acute{\eta}s$—كاذب—כוזב). For truth is the correspondence of what is conceived with what is perceived. To express this distinction between a true and a false idea we either affirm or deny of a thing its existence outside the mind. The test of such existence is knowledge, direct or indirect. Of a true idea we, therefore, affirm that it is directly perceived or otherwise known to agree with reality. Now, in the Arabic language, says

מציאות בלא מהות ולא מחות בלא מציאות; ואמום האמינו שהמציאות במורכב תואר נוסף על עצמותו, ושזה התאר אמנם קנאו מהפועל, והאמינו במה שהוא פשוט שזה התאר לו אינו נוסף על המהות, ושהוא אין לו מהות מתחלף למציאות, לא שהוא אין לו מהות בלל כמו שכנה הוא כלל דבורו בסתירדתם (הפלת ההפלת, שאלה ח').

That these two formulas represent two distinct theories, would also seem to follow from this passage of Thomas Aquinas's *De ente et essentia*. ' Aliquid enim est, sicut Deus, cuius essentia est ipsum suum esse ; et ideo inveniuntur *aliqui philosophi* dicentes quod Deus non habet essentiam, quia essentia eius non est aliud quam esse eius.' As to who the *aliqui philosophi* were, Cajetan identifies them with the Platonists, a term, as has been observed, used by him loosely to indicate some gnostic sect (cf. *De ente et essentia*, ed. Émile Bruneteau, Paris, 1914, p. 114, note 1). It is more probable that Thomas refers there to Algazali. Professor Maurice De Wulf, however, was kind enough to advise me that in his opinion the phrase *aliqui philosophi* refers to some contemporary teachers in the University of Paris and not necessarily to some well-known philosophers.

Averroes, the same root وجد, 'to find', which signifies the essential existence, means also to find out the presence of something by means of the senses or of the intellect. Thus 'God is existent' means that God is perceived or known to have objective reality corresponding to our subjective idea of Him. In the proposition 'centaurs are not existent' we likewise mean to deny the perception of centaurs to agree with our conception thereof. In either case, however, ideal existence is identical with essence.[86]

The same difference of opinion between Avicenna and Averroes recurs with regard to the attribute of unity.

[86] Cf. Narboni's Commentary on Algazali's *Intentions*, Metaphysics, Part I.

וכתב אבן רשד, זה לשונו: מעות אבן סינא, שהוא בעבור שראה שם הנמצא מורה על הצודק בדבור הערבי והיה אשר מורה על הצורך מורה על מקרה בלי ספק, אבל גם באמתות על מושכל מן המושכלות השניות, רצוני לומר, הדבריות, חשב שכאשר עשאהו המעתיקים אמנם יורה על זה הענין, ואין הענין כן. אבל אמנם כונו בו המעתיקים שיורו בו על אשר יורה עליו שם העצמות והדבר. וכבר באר זה אבונצר בספר האותיות, וידע שאחת מסבות הטעות הנופלות בזה הוא ששם הנמצא הוא בתנועה נגזר, והנגזר יורה על מקרה, אבל הוא בשרש הלשון נגזר, אלא שהמעתיקים אחר שלא מצאו בלשון הערב תיבה מורה על זה הענין, אשר היו הקודמים חולקים אותו אל העצם והמקרה, ואל הכח והפעל, רצוני לומר, תיבה היא המשל ראשון, הורו עליו קצתם בשם הנמצא, לא על שיובן ממנו ענין הגזרת, ויורה על מקרה, אבל ענין אשר יורה עליו שם העצמות, והוא כל דבר הוה, והוא שם מלאכותיי, לא לשוניי ע"כ.

But Aristotle himself, as is well known, distinguishes four different usages of the term τὸ ὄν, two of which correspond to those mentioned by Averroes, namely, (1) in the sense of truth and falsehood (Τὸ ὂν λέγεται τὸ μὲν κατὰ συμβεβηκός), (2) that which is divided into the categories ("Ἔτι τὸ εἶναι σημαίνει καὶ τὸ ἔστιν ὅτι ἀληθές, τὸ δὲ μὴ εἶναι ὅτι οὐκ ἀληθὲς ἀλλὰ ψεῦδος) (cf. Metaphysics, IV, 7, V, 2; Grote, *Aristotle*, vol. I, chap. III). Thus it is not altogether the translator's fault that Avicenna confused the two meanings of the term (see the interpretation of Averroes' criticism given by Munk, *Guide*, vol. I, p. 231).

Here, again, for similar reasons Avicenna maintains that, like existence, unity is only accidental to essence. Averroes, on the contrary, maintains that unity is identical with essence, but distinguishing between absolute and numerical unity, he admits the latter to be accidental, and it is this accidental kind of unity that is always referred to in propositions affirming unity.

Among Jewish philosophers, Maimonides and his immediate disciples [87] followed Avicenna. All later Jewish thinkers accepted the view of Averroes.[88] Having a new theory of his own, Crescas undertakes to expose the untenability of both the old systems.

Whatever the meaning of existence with respect to creatures may be, contends Crescas, with respect to God it is generally admitted, by both the Avicennean and the Averroesean groups, that existence is identical with the divine essence. Hence it must be inferred that they all interpret the attribute of existence homonymously, for as there is no relation between the divine and the created essence, so there cannot be any relation between their

[87] Cf. *Drei Abhandlungen von Josef b. Jehuda* (מאמר ר׳ יוסף ב״ר יהודה תלמיד הרמב״ם), edited by Moritz Löwy, Berlin, 1879, Hebrew text, p. 15.

[88] Cf. commentaries on the *Moreh*, as well as the commentaries of Narboni and Albalag on Algazali's *Intentions*. Cf. also Albo's *Ikkarim*, II, ch. I. Narboni, in his commentary on the *Intentions*, after quoting at length Averroes' arguments against Avicenna, adds the following remark: 'I have dwelt rather too long on this subject, because I have noticed that the savant, our Master Moses [i. e. Maimonides], following Algazali and Avicenna, had begun one of his chapters by saying that "existence is an accident superadded to the existent being". Would that that statement had not existed.'

והארכתי בבאור זה; למה שראיתי החכם רבינו משה נמשך בספריו אחר דעת אבו חמד ואבן סינא בזה, עד שהתחיל בפרק מפרקיו, המציאות מקרה קרה לנמצא, ומי יתן ולא נמצא.

existences. Consequently, queries Crescas, 'Would that I could conceive what is the significance of the term existence when applied to God, for our affirmation that God is existent, in which the latter term is not different from the former, is tantamount to our saying that God is God'.[89] Two inaccuracies of this argument of Crescas must not be passed over unnoticed. In the first place the inference that the homonymous interpretation of the term existence must follow its identification with the divine essence, is erroneous. Gersonides, for instance, follows Averroes in the identification of essence and existence, and still interprets the latter ambiguously, according to the distinction of priority and posteriority.[90] In the second place, in interpreting existence homonymously Maimonides circumvents the objection of tautology by taking it as an emphasis of the negation of non-existence.[91]

But the objection may be urged even with regard to created existences if we accept the view of Averroes and his followers, who consider existence to be nothing but the essence. For, according to this view, the proposition 'man is existent' or 'white is existent' would be equivalent to saying 'man is man' or 'white is white'.[92] This criticism is neither original nor irrefutable. In fact, it is the very same argument that had been advanced by Algazali in support of the Avicennean theory of the distinction between existence and essence.[93] Again, Averroes's refutation

[89] *Or Adonai*, I, III, 1, p. 21 b–22 a.
[90] Cf. *Milhamot*, V, III, 12, p. 46 b, and III, 3, p. 23 a.
[91] Cf. *Moreh*, I, 58.   [92] *Or Adonai*, I, III, 1, p. 22 a.
[93] Cf. Algazali's *Intentions*, Metaphysics: In refutation of the view that existence and essence are identical, he says: 'This is refutable on two grounds: first, when we say the substance is existent it is evidently a proposition conjoined of two terms. Now if the existence of the substance

thereof, based upon a distinction in the use of the term existence, was well known and had been quoted by all the commentators on the *Moreh*.[94]

The view held by Avicenna that existence is only accidental to the essence, says Crescas, is still less tenable. The term accident had been used by Avicenna in two senses, a general and a specific.[95] In its general sense the term is applied to everything which requires a subject of inhesion. In its specific sense, however, it is applied only to those that require a subject of inhesion, and of which the subject of inhesion is independent, as, for instance, *white* and *cloth*. Form, therefore, though an accident in the general meaning, having no existence apart from matter, is not an accident in the specific meaning of the term, since Matter in its turn has no subsistence without Form. And so Form is included among the four Substances. It is with reference to these two meanings of the term accident, if I am not mistaken, that Crescas urges the next two arguments against Avicenna's accidental interpretation of

were the essence of it, our statement would assert that substance is substance.'

... וזה נפסד משני פנים, אחד מהם, שאמרנו העצם נמצא דבור
מחובר סובן, ולו היה מציאות העצם עין העצם, היה כאמרנו העצם עצם.

[94] Cf. *supra*, notes 84 and 86.

[95] Cf. Algazali's *Intentions*, Metaphysics, I. He divides there existence (מציאות) into two classes; one, which needs an abode (משכן) as accidents (מקרים), and another, which has no need for an abode. Those which need an abode are again divided into two classes: one, where the abode is independent of the accident, and, another, where the abode is dependent upon the accident. In the former case the accident bears the name accident (מקרה), whereas the abode is called the subject (נושא). In the latter case the accident is called *Form* (צורה) whereas the abode is called ὕλη (היולי). In fact the inclusion of the Form among the Substances is opposed by the Mutakallemim, who consider it as a mere accident dependent upon its abode (cf. *Moreh*, I, 73, proposition 8).

existence. Assuming at first that by interpreting existence as an accident Avicenna uses the term accident in its specific sense, Crescas attempts to reduce that view to an absurdity.[96] If anything, said to be existent, has its existence added to its essence, that existence, which we may designate as primary, being merely an accident, cannot be self-subsistent. In compliance with the definition of accident it must have existence in something else. Thus accidental primary existence will have accidental secondary existence. By analogous reasoning the secondary existence will need to have tertiary, and so the process may go on *ad infinitum*.[97]

---

[96] *Or Adonai*, I, III, 1, p. 22 a. 'No less a difficulty may be pointed out in the view of him who states that existence in all other beings is outside the essence to which the former is superadded as an accident. For if existence is an accident it must have a subject of inhesion, and thus existence will have existence. If the other existence is also an accident, that, too, will require a subject of inhesion and thus will have a still other existence, and so on to infinity.'

[97] This argument had been anticipated by many authors. Joseph Ben Judah, Ibn Aknin, a disciple of Maimonides, both raises and answers this objection (cf. *Drei Abhandlungen von Josef b. Jehuda*, von Moritz Löwy, Berlin, 1879, Hebrew text, p. 15:

ואם נאמר באשר היה המציאות תאר לנמצא הנה הוא תאר נמצא, הנה הוא נמצא במציאות וכן יהיה זה המציאות נמצא במציאות, וילך הענין אל בלתי תכלית).

It is also found in Albalag's commentary on the *Intentions*, Metaphysics:

אם תאמר שהוא [כלומר, תאר המציאות] נוסף, יתחייב שיהיה למציאות מציאות, ולמציאות מציאות, וכן עד בלתי תכלית.

The argument is also found in Aegidius's *De esse et essentia*, which had been translated into Hebrew at about the middle of the fourteenth century (Jews' College, London, 268):

א״כ צריך שכל דבר שישותו הוא דבר ממבעו, יהיה לו הישות מדבר אחר, ובעבור שהישות, שהוא כולל דבר אחר, יובא אל אותו הישות שהוא בעצמו, כמו שיובא העלול לסבה הראשונה, צריך שיהיה דבר אחר

If you say, as had been really suggested by Algazali, that existence, like Form, is an accident only in the general acceptation of the term, on account of its dependence upon essence, but again like Form it is a substance, and thus capable of self-subsistence, the question is, Why should existence be called accident any more than Form, since both, though accidents in the general sense of the term, are not accidents in its specific sense?[98] Thus, existence can be neither identical with the essence nor accidental to it.

Nor can unity be identical with or accidental to the essence. The arguments employed here by Crescas are merely a repetition of those employed by him in the case of existence. There is, however, one novel argument. Quoting the commonly accepted definition of unity as the negation of diversity, he continues: 'and if we say that unity, signifying the absence of plurality, is identical with

שיהיה סבת הישות לכל הנמצאים, בעבור שהוא ישות לבד, ועל תכונה אחרת היתה החליבה בסבות לבלתי תכלית.

Likewise Gersonides urges the same argument against the accidentality of unity, which he says may also be applied to the accidentality of existence; cf. *Milḥamot*, V, 12.

ועוד שאם היה כל דבר אחד מצד מקרה מה נמצא בו, הנה יחוייב בזה המקרה כשהודיעו עליו בשם בלתי נגזר, שיחיה מתואר בשהוא אחד מצד מקרה אחר נמצאנו בו, וילך אל לא תכלית . . . . . ולזאת הסבה נ"כ נאמר שעצם כל דבר נמצא, ר"ל, שלא יורה הנמצא עליו מצד מקרה נוסף על המהות.

[98] 'Furthermore, existence is like Form in its relation to Matter, since, according to their contention, without that accident [i.e. existence] the subject would have been nonexistent. And so, since that accident bestows existence and permanency upon the substance, it deserves to be called Substance prior to the subject, just as Form is called Substance prior to Matter, as it has been stated in the *Physics*, Book I. But existence is called by them accident, which is an incorrigible contradiction.'

the essence of the object predicated by one, it would follow that all objects described by one are one in essence'.[99] This argument may be easily identified as the application of the well-known mediaeval argument against the identity theory of universals as well as against monopsychism.[100]

CHAPTER III

Crescas's Theory of Attributes.

It would be comparatively easy and not altogether unjustifiable to dismiss Crescas's theory of attributes as a conglomeration of incongruous statements. Such, indeed, was the verdict passed upon it by an early critic.[101] The difficulties which one encounters in the attempt to give a constructive presentation of his view are many. Besides the lack of coherence and definiteness in his exposition, Crescas seems radically to contradict himself. Starting out to prove that divine attributes are positive, upon getting embroiled in the inevitable difficulties consequent to such a thesis, without much ado Crescas quite unostentatiously concludes that after all some of the attributes are negative

---

[99] *Or Adonai*, I, III, 3, p. 22 b.

[100] Cf. Gersonides, *Milḥamot*, V, 12. 'For if unity were a genus it could not be predicated of the *differentiae* by which the species which are included under it are classified, for the genus cannot be predicated of the *differentiae* by which its subordinate species are classified. For example, animality is not predicable of rationality and volatility.'

שאם היה האחד סוג, היה בלתי אפשר שינשא האחד על ההבדלים אשר יחלקו בהם המינים אשר יקוף בהם, והמשל כי החי לא ינשא על הדבור והעופפות.

[101] Cf. Abraham Shalom's *Neveh Shalom*, XII, I, 3. 'It is surprising how that author changes his view in an instant.'

ומהפלא מזה החכם ומסברתו ההפוכה כמו רגע.

in meaning. If negativity is to be the ultimate solution of some of the attributes, it had been asked, why should it not be equally applied to all the attributes, and what is then the meaning of all his contentions against Maimonides?[102] This inconsistency, however, is too apparent to be real, and the absence of any explanation on the part of the author of what appears to be an abrupt reversal of his own position, leads us at least to suspect whether his final statement does really reverse his original thesis. While we do not hold a brief for the author, defending him against his critics as to the adequacy of his justification of positive essential attributes, we shall, however, endeavour to give a constructive and consistent view of his attempt to do so.

If the problem of attributes, as I have attempted to show in the first chapter, is in its final analysis a question as to the relation of the universal essence to the individual; in order to understand Crescas's position on attributes we must first construct his theory of universals. Suggestions available for the construction of his theory of universals are abundant. He differs with both Avicenna and Averroes, and with the latter more than with the former. Admitting with Avicenna that the universal substance is distinct from the individual, he differs with him as to the relation between these two. According to Avicenna,

---

[102] Cf. *ibid.*, XII, I, 4. 'This author has just stated that existence means not nonexistence, and that unity means the absence of plurality. How then could he have said, just an instant before, that existence and unity are essential attributes?'

והנה החכם הזה הוא האומר שהמציאות יורה על היותו בלתי נעדר,
והאחדות על היותו בזולת רבוי, ואיך היה דעתו לשמה כרגע לומר
שהנמצא והאחד תארים עצמיים.

while the universal does not exist apart from the individual, nor the individual apart from the universal, they can both at least be thought of as separate existences. But Crescas insists upon their mutual interdependence in thought. Differentiated in thought though they are, still in thought they are inseparable. Not only cannot rationality or animality be conceivable without the individual human essence, but likewise the individual human essence cannot be conceived without the universal conceptions of rationality and animality. Such 'essential universals', he says, are 'conditions' of the individual essences, not mere mental abstractions or inventions, but real entities, so united as not to be distinguishable except by thought; but they are also so mutually implicative as not to be thought of one without the other.

What essential universals, which form the definition, are to the individual essence of the defined object, all the attributes are to the divine essence, and they are positive. But before proceeding any further let us explain the special sense in which Crescas uses the term positive attribute. Positive attribute may mean two things. In the first place it means the existence of qualities distinct from the essence. In the second place, it means that any predicate affirmed of God is used in a sense not entirely unrelated to its original, ordinary meaning. In Hebrew the same word (תאר) is used in these two senses. In English, however, we may call the one 'attribute' and the other 'predicate'. Now, in the different theories of attributes which we have analysed in a previous chapter, the main controversy was not about the 'attributes', but rather about the 'predicates'. Both Maimonides and Gersonides admit that God does not possess any attributes distinct from His essence. Their reasons, however, vary. The former maintains that in this respect God is absolutely different from other beings, whereas the latter believes that even in created beings essential universals are not distinguishable from the individual essence except in name. And so, while both deny the distinction of essence and 'attribute' within the divine substance, Maimonides interprets the 'predicates' as negatives, that is to say, as homonymous terms, but Gersonides interprets them as positives, that is to say, as ambiguous terms applied to God and to other beings in a related sense, *secundum prius et posterius*. Now, Crescas, as we shall see, endeavours to prove that attributes are positive both in the sense that the divine substance is composed of essence and attribute, and in the sense that the predicate affirmed of God is a related term. This, however, does not mean to say that every single attribute is positive in both these senses. If it can be shown that a certain attribute, even in its application to other beings, has no positive meaning, it can still be called positive predicate, because of its being applied to God and to other beings in a related sense. In the proposition A is X, for instance, let us say that X means $-Y$. If we then affirm that 'God is X', using here X in the same sense as in the proposition 'A is X', we may then say that X in its application to God is a positive predicate, even though its meaning is negative. 'Positive' in this sense would not refer at all to the *positive content* of the term employed as the predicate of the proposition; it would rather refer to the *positive relation* of the content of the term in its application to God, to the content of the same term in its application to other beings, the content itself being either positive or negative.

Of all the attributes, existence and unity stand out as

a class by themselves. They are to every individual essence what its essential universals by which it is defined are to it. Man, for instance, besides his two essential universals, animality and rationality, and his many adventitious qualities, has also the two attributes existence and unity, which like the former are inseparable from his essence. For existence and unity are conditions of thought, without which nothing is conceivable. 'Every essence must unconditionally have objective reality outside the mind',[103] which is the meaning of existence; and every such actually existent substance must be one and limited.[104]

The relation that commonly obtains between the attributes of existence and unity and every individual essence, likewise holds true between both these attributes and the divine essence. As to the meaning of existence, however, there are two phases, a general and a specific. The general meaning is negative and invariable, but the specific meaning is positive and subject to variations. The general meaning of existence is non-subjectivity; that of unity is non-plurality. In that sense, each of these attributes is invariably applied, without any shade of difference, to accidents, substances, and God. The specific meaning of existence, however, is objectivity, and the specific meaning of unity is simplicity. In this positive phase each of these attributes is applied in different degrees to accidents, substances, and God. Substances are more objective than

---

[103] *Or Adonai*, I, III, 1, p. 22 a.

וזה שמתנאי המהות היותו נמצא חוץ לשכל.

and cf. quotation in note 105.

[104] *Ibid.*, I, III, 3, p. 22 b.

ולזה הוא מבואר שאין היחוד . . . אלא דבר עצמי לכל הנמצא בפועל ומוגבל.

and cf. quotation in note 105.

accidents, since the latter have no reality except as part of the former. Likewise, substances are more simple than accidents, since the latter, again, are divisible not only by their own potentiality, but also by that of their subject of inhesion. And than both God is more real and more simple in a superlative degree.[105]

All other attributes, however, that with respect to created beings are only accidental, differ in their application to God not only in degree but also in the manner of their relation to His essence, for all the divine attributes are inseparable and essential. Crescas especially mentions the attributes of Priority, Knowledge, and Power. Priority implies time, and time is an accident related to motion in all created being, and is subject to the variation of more or less. With respect to God, however, it is essential and

[105] *Ibid.*, I, III, 1, p. 22 a. 'It has thus been shown by an irrefutable argument that existence cannot be accidental to the essence. It must therefore be either identical with the essence itself or essential to it. Since it cannot be the essence itself, as it has been shown in the first argument, it must be essential to it, that is to say, that it is one of the conditions of the essence to exist outside the mind. Just as animality and rationality are said to be the human essence, so it is one of the conditions of the essence to have extra-mental existence. And so the term existence is applied univocally to all beings that are not prior to one another, that is, excluding accidents. Of substances and accidents, therefore, the term is applied ambiguously, since extramental existence is primarily applied to substance and through it subsequently to accidents. The general meaning, however, is that whatever is predicated by existence is not absent. It is in this sense of non-absence that the term is applied to God and to other substances, except that to God it is applied primarily and to other beings subsequently. It is thus clear that the term existence in its application to God and to other beings is not a perfect homonym, but it is a certain kind of ambiguity' [i. e. *secundum prius et posterius*]. Cf. also *ibid.*, I, III, 1, p. 22 b. 'It is thus clear that unity is not the essence itself . . . . . . nor anything added to the essence. It is something essential to everything that is actually existent and limited, and is a mental distinction with respect to the absence of plurality.' Cf. Ḥobot ha-Lebabot, I, 8.

inseparable as if it were His definition. Furthermore, it is used in a superlative sense; thus acquiring the meaning of first, eternal, or rather that of uncreated. The same holds also true of Knowledge and Power. In created beings they are acquired and accidental; in God they are inseparably essential. Again, in created beings they are each in a limited degree, in God they are in the highest degree possible. Thus all the divine attributes are ambiguous, but not homonymous terms. While they differ from their ordinary usage in degree, or in both degree and relation to essence, they all share in common their primary meaning. Existence, unity, priority, knowledge, and power, in their application to God, are in their primary meaning related to the corresponding terms in their application to created beings.[106]

But would not that relation imply similarity? Crescas tries to answer this question as follows: Related terms are similar, when the relation has some numerical value; that is to say, when the related terms are both finite. When one of the terms, however, is infinite, its relation to a finite term has no numerical value, and hence they are dissimilar. The divine attributes, as has been stated, are used in a superlative degree. His knowledge is infinite, and so are all his other attributes. Thus, while they are related in meaning to created attributes, their relation has no numerical value, whence it does not imply similarity.[107]

[106] Cf. *supra* quotations in note 105.

[107] *Ibid.*, I, III, 3, pp. 23 b-24 a. 'We say, there is no doubt that any similarity between God and His creatures must be dismissed as impossible. Still, though the perfection [attributed to God and to His creatures] belong to the same genus, there is no similarity between them, since they are so widely distinguished whether with respect to necessity and possibility of existence or with respect to finitude and infinity. This is the meaning

There is another difficulty which Crescas endeavours to obviate. 'It is now imperative upon us', he says, 'to explain why the negation of essential attributes does not necessarily follow our acceptance of the proposition that everything that is composed of two elements cannot be necessary existence.' This difficulty presents itself in two ways. First, since there are many attributes, each of which is distinct from all others, it would follow that the attribute part of God, which is not unidentical with but is inseparable from His essence, would have to be composite. Second, the aggregate of those attributes taken as a whole, being distinct from the divine essence, would together with that essence imply a plurality in the divine substance. With regard to the first, Crescas maintains that all the attributes are mental modifications of the single attribute of Goodness. Though not identical with goodness, all the other attributes cannot be separated from it even in thought. The relation, therefore, of the individual attributes to the general goodness is similar to that of the attribute as a whole to the essence.[108] It is this mental inseparability which makes

of the verse "To whom then will ye liken God? or what likeness will ye compare unto Him?" [Isa. 40. 18]. The prophet thereby explains that only that kind of similarity is forbidden to attribute to God which implies a certain comparison. But as the alleged similarity between God and His creatures is incomparable, for there can be no relation and also comparison between the infinite and the finite, there is no implication of real similarity in the affirmation of attributes.'

[108] That the relation of the individual attributes to Goodness is, according to Crescas, similar to the relation of Goodness, or the totality of attributes, to the essence, may be inferred from the following passage: 'Just as essence cannot be conceived without existence nor existence without essence, so the attribute cannot be conceived without its subject nor the subject without its attribute. And all the attributes are likewise comprehended in absolute goodness, which is the sum total of all perfections'. *Or Adonai*, I, III, 3, p. 25 b.

them all one. In this, indeed, he follows Maimonides' explanation of the plurality of divine activities, with only the following two exceptions. Maimonides takes intelligence as the unifying principle, whereas Crescas takes goodness; and, again, Maimonides considers all other activities as different aspects of intelligence which are in reality identical with it, whereas Crescas considers the other attributes to be distinct from goodness. Upon the fundamental difference between intelligence and goodness more will be said later on.[109] With regard to the second, Crescas maintains that the mental distinction between essence and attribute is not contradictory to the conception of necessary existence, since they are inseparable in thought. Necessary existence excludes composition only in so far as that composition would necessitate an external agent by which that existence would have been rendered conditional. Such would be the case if the divine substance were conceived to consist of parts which could in any way be separately conceived of. But in the divine substance the attributes and the essence cannot be thought of one without the other, just as the essence and the radiative quality of a luminous object cannot be thought of separately. It is the possibility of being separately conceived and not the mere fact of a mental distinction that militates against necessary existence.[110] This answer, however, concludes Crescas, must be resorted to only in the case of attributes whose primary meaning is positive, as, for instance, Power and Knowledge. There are some attri-

[109] In the chapters on Crescas's theory of Divine Omniscience and the Purpose of the Universe which are not included in this thesis.

[110] This line of reasoning sounds like a modified and moderated restatement of Algazali's definition of absolute simplicity (cf. *supra*, chap. I, note 38 and chap. II, note 70).

butes whose positive meaning in the final analysis is nothing but a negation. The positive meaning of Existence, for instance, is nothing but a mental antithesis of absence; that of unity is a mental antithesis of plurality; that of priority when applied in a superlative sense of infinite priority comes to mean not-having-been-created, which is eternity, and in its final analysis, the absence of temporal relation. Though these attributes, too, are applied to God in the same positive sense as to created beings, their positive sense, however, in both cases is only a negation.[111]

[111] *Or Adonai*, I, III, 3, p. 24 b. 'It is now left for us to explain that the negation of essential attributes must not necessarily follow the accepted proposition which states that whatever is composite cannot have necessary existence. The explanation of this is not difficult, and it may be stated in two ways. First, though with respect to ourselves the attributes are separate, with respect to God they are unified. The infinite goodness which is essential to God comprehends all the attributes rendering them one. Second, that proposition is true only under a certain condition, namely, when the joined and composite object is such that it requires an agent to perform its composition as, for instance, when each part of the composition is part of its essence, in which case we must say that the composition brought about by the composing agent is the cause of the composite object. But the Blessed One has no divided substance, for His substance is simple in an absolute sense, and goodness in general follows from him essentially. Why, then, is it impossible that God should be necessary existence by His essence even though goodness in general or infinite knowledge, power, and the other perfections in particular, follow from Him essentially, just as light could have eradiated from a luminous object, even if that object were assumed to be necessary existence by its essence? Would the assumption of necessary existence render the radiation of the light impossible? No! For the light is not something essentially different from the substance of the luminous object, and thus does not require an external agent to bring about its composition with the latter; it is rather something essential to the luminous object and appropriately predicable thereof. That is exactly the meaning of divine attrributes. So much the more the attribute *priority* which is a mental distinction of His not having been created, *existence* which is an indication of His

This would seem entirely to dispose of the negative interpretation of Attributes. The burden of authority, however, weighed heavily, and while Crescas dared disagree with Maimonides, for which there had been many precedents, he could not completely ignore the views of Ibn Gabirol, Judah Halevi, Baḥya Ibn Pekudah, and others, all of whom had incorporated the negative interpretation in their respective solutions of the problem of attributes. To avoid this predicament, Crescas interprets the texts of those authors so as to harmonize with his own view. His interpretation is based upon the distinction we have already pointed out between the two usages of the Hebrew word תאר, one meaning 'attribute', the other 'predicate'. The existence of essential attributes in the divine being, says Crescas, had never been denied by the ancients. They had only maintained that some 'predicates' must be interpreted negatively, and those, too, only in the case when the predicates denote the essence itself. God, however, possesses essential attributes, and terms connoting those attributes are not to be taken as negatives. In the words of the author: 'We must, therefore, say that whenever some of the savants exclude the positive meaning of attributes, interpreting them all as negations, they must be understood to refer only to such predicates as describe the essence itself. These alone cannot be taken in a positive sense. And note this distinction.'[112]

Thus the divine being consists of an essence and essential attributes, the unity of the former being preserved by the

not being absent, and *unity* which indicates that there is no plurality in His essence and that in no way does He contain any duality.'

[112] *Or Adonai*, I, III, ४, p. 26 a :

ולזה צריך שנאמר שאם היו קצת החכמים . . .

mental inseparability of its parts. This view, says Crescas, is in conformity with the following statement which is found in the mystic writing called the Book of Creation. 'The manner in which the flame is united with the coal is an illustration of the irruptible unity.'[113] The implication of this statement, continues he, is as follows: 'Just as essence cannot be conceived without existence nor existence without essence, so the attribute cannot be conceived without its subject nor the subject without its attribute; and all the attributes are comprehended in absolute goodness, which is the sum total of all perfections.'[114] It is due to their failure to distinguish inseparable essential attributes from separable attributes that the philosophers, and especially Maimonides, were compelled to reject the existence of divine attributes altogether. To them only two alternatives presented themselves, either attributes are identical with the essence or they are different from it, in the latter case implying plurality. That attributes may be unidentical with the essence and still both together be one, they failed to perceive. A similar error was made by them in their theory of knowledge. Finding it impossible to conceive the subject, object, and process of knowing as different things, they were forced to declare them all identical—

[113] *Ibid.*, I, III, 3, p. 25 b. The text of the *Sefer Yeṣira* is paraphrased by Crescas. Originally the passage reads as follows: 'Their end [i. e. of the Ten Sefirot] is inserted in their beginning, and their beginning in their end, even as the flame is joined to the coal. Know, think, and imagine, that the Lord is one and the Creator is one, and there is no second to that oneness, and before one what number can you name?'

נעוץ סופן בתחלתן, ותחלתן בסופן, כשלהבת קשורה בנחלת, דע
וחשוב וצור שאדון יחיד והיוצר אחד, ואין שני לו, ולפני אחד מה
אתה סופר ?

(cf. *Sefer Yeṣira*, Goldschmidt's edition, p. 51).

[114] *Ibid.*

a view which is untenable for many reasons. But there, too, 'the philosophers tripped and fell because they did not distinguish the essential from the identical'.[115] The *ens intelligens* is not identical with the *intellectus*, but is essential to and inseparable from it. Attributes are, therefore, positive, and have their real counterpart in the divine being. With this the knowability of God is no longer impossible. His essence, to be sure, can never be known; His essential attributes, however, can be comprehended.

While to Crescas the compatibility of essential attributes with absolute existence and unity seemed clear and indisputable, his position has not escaped cavilling criticism. It has indeed been charged to be open to the same objection that in his *Refutation of the Christian Principles*[116] Crescas himself had pointed out in the Christian doctrine of the Trinity. The type of trinitarian doctrine which Crescas deals with in his polemic is, generally speaking, that of the Western Church, though as to its identification with any specific creed I am not in a position to express an opinion.[117] He outlines it as follows. The divine substance or Godhead consists of one essence and three

[115] *Or Adonai*, IV, 11, p. 91 a.

[116] Cf. בטול עקרי הנוצרים, originally written in Spanish, and translated into Hebrew by Joseph b. Shemtob.

[117] Professor George Foot Moore was kind enough to make the following observation. 'The peculiar definition of the Christian theory of the Trinity which you find in Crescas is also to be found in Ramban's Disputation with the controvertite Pablo before King James of Aragon, in 1263, the text of which was printed by Wagenseil in a volume under the title *Tela Ignea Satanae*, 1681. The passage is near the end of the Disputation. Ramban gives for the three persons of the Trinity, החכמה והחפץ והיכולת. I take that Crescas's רצון, and Ramban's חפץ are equivalent, not to *voluntas*, but *benignitas*, or *caritas*, i. e. not "will" but "good-will". In this form, Power, Wisdom, Good-Will, we have the theory of the Trinity set forth by Abelard (died 1142), which was condemned by a synod at Soissons, in 1121.'

distinct personalities, Father, Son, and Holy Ghost, correspondingly respectively to the attributes of Power, Wisdom, and Will. The Personalities are not identical with the essence. The Personalities, furthermore, are distinct from each other, and are interrelated as cause and effect, the Father being the cause of the Son, and these two of the Holy Ghost. Again, the Personalities are the causes of their respectively corresponding three attributes. Finally, the three Personalities are co-equal, all of them being Gods.[118] In his criticism, Crescas chiefly assails that part of the doctrine which maintains the distinctness of the Personalities from the essence, showing that conception to be at variance with divine unity.[119] But according to the testimony of the translator, Isaac ben Shemtob, the same arguments that Crescas had urged against the distinctness of the Personalities were urged by others against his own theory of divine attributes. 'I have noticed', he says, 'that some scholars had raised the same difficulties with respect to our author's theory of divine attributes.'[120] The trans-

[118] הפ' הג' בשלוש. האמונה הנוצרית מנחת שהעצם האלהי יכלל על ג' תארים, פירשונאש [persones] בלשונם, ומהות אחד: אב, בן, ורוח הקודש יבולת, חכמה, ורצון. האב מוליד הבן, ומאהבת שניהם הרוה"ק הוא נאצל. מהאב הוא היכולת, מהבן הוא החכמה, מהרוח הרצון. והג' במהות אלה אל אחד, הם נבדלים אבל בתארים. וכל אחד מהם הוא אלוה. זאת היא אמונתם בזה העקר (Ibid.)

[119] והעקר הג' הוא השלוש . . . . . ההקדמות המתחלפות ג': א', שהנוצרי אומר שיש בעל ית' ג' תוארים נבדלים, בלשונם פריסונאש, והיהודי כופר בזה. ב', שהנוצרי מאמין שיש באל ית' תאר נקרא בן נולד מאב, והיהודי כופר בזה. ג', שהנוצרי מאמין שיש באל ית' תאר נאצל מהאב והבן נקרא רוח, והיהודי כופר בכל (Ibid.)

[120] והוצרכתי להעירך עליו, יען כי ראיתי קצת משכילים ישבו על סברת זה החכם, בהאמינו חתארים העצמיים, קצת מאלה הבמולים (Ibid.)

lator, however, comes to Crescas's defence by pointing out a radical distinction between personalities and attributes, namely, that the former being causatively interrelated are necessarily many, whereas the latter are absolutely unified by absolute goodness.[121]

The abstruseness of Crescas's reconciliation of essential attributes with absolute unity has also been pointed out by Abraham Shalom in his *Dwelling of Peace*.[122] 'We may ask the author [i. e. Crescas] as follows: Are there essential attributes identical with the essence or added to it? for these are the only two possible alternatives. If he says that they are identical, he has gained nothing by interpreting Moses' prayer to refer to essential attributes.... If he says that these attributes, though distinct with respect to ourselves, are one with respect to God, then it must mean that they are identical.... If the author retorts that the essential Attributes are indistinguishable from the essence except in thought, we may ask him again: Are they conceived in

[121] אמר יוסף, דרוש התארים עמוק מאד .... והרב הזה החזיק בתארים העצמיים ... אבל ראוי שתדע שהמקיים התארים העצמיים איננו תחת זה הסוג, ואנחנו לא מצאנו מלה אחרת יותר נאותה בהעתקה למלת פריסונה זולת התאר, אבל אין מבנם אחד. זה מבואר. שהם אמרו שהאב המוליד הבן. ומי שמניח שבו ית' יכולת והחכמה לא יחשוב חלילה שהיכולת יפעל לחכמה, ולא שהיכולת אלוה, והחכמה אלוה (.Ibid)

[122] Cf. *Neveh Shalom*, XII, I, 3:

נשאל לחכם ונאמר, אם אלה התארים העצמיים הם עצמותו, אם הם נוסף על עצמותו, שזה חלוקה חכרחית. אם יאמר שהם עצמותו, א"כ לא הרויח דבר בהניחו בקשת משה רבינו ע"ה התארים העצמיים .... אם יאמר שהתארים האלת, עם היותם נבדלים בחקנו, הם מתאחדים בחקו, אם כן גם עצמותו .... ואם יענה זה החכם שחשנת תאריו העצמיים הם בחינות שכליות, נשאלהו מאותם הבחינות, האם יובחנו בבח השכל היותם עצם או מקרה, וישוב הספק הא' למקומו, ואין לדבר סוף.

thought to be essential or accidental? and thus we land again on the horns of our previous dilemma, and so we may go on asking and answering like that *ad infinitum.*' The main point of this criticism, as it may be gathered, is that if things are one they must be identical, and if they are not identical they cannot be one. To take an object which is physically one, and call it two, because it is so conceived in thought, and then call it one again, because its parts are inseparable in thought, is past comprehension.

Another derogatory reference to Crescas's theory of attributes is found in Abrabanel's commentary on the *Moreh*. In his discussion of Attributes, Maimonides cites the view of a certain class of thinkers who had held that besides those attributes, which must be either identical with the essence or accidental to it, there are some which 'are neither His essence nor anything extraneous to his essence'. Dismissing this view as an utter absurdity, Maimonides remarks that 'it exists only in words, not in thought, much less in reality'; and that 'if a man were to examine for himself his own belief on the subject, he would see nothing but confusion and stupidity in an endeavour to prove the existence of things that do not exist, or to find a means between two opposites that have no means'. Commenting upon this passage, Abrabanel makes the statement that this view, which had been spurned by Maimonides, was afterwards taken up by Crescas.[123]

The influence of Crescas's theory of divine attributes

[123] Cf. Abrabanel's commentary on the *Moreh*, I, 51:

אחרי שבטל הרב היות התארים עצמו . . . . ולא שיהיו יוצאים
מעצמו . . . . זכר דעת ג', שהיה אצל קצת המדברים, שאמרו שהתארים
המתוארים בו ית' אינם עצמו ואינם מקרה יוצא מעצמו, אבל הם דברים
עצמיים בו, וזהו דעת הר' חסדאי במ"א מספרו.

may be traced in the *Principles*[124] of his pupil Joseph Albo. Albo's theory of attributes is eclectic rather than systematic, and Crescas's view is partly adapted by him as a prerequisite of his conception of necessary existence. Necessary existence, according to Albo, implies four conditions: unity, incorporeality, timelessness, and indeficiency;[125] a classification which, it must be observed, overlaps and could not stand the test of a logical analysis. The first of these conditions excludes separable attributes, both accidental and essential; the second excludes bodily emotions; the third, by inference, negates relation and similarity; the fourth rejects any implication of deficiency. Accordingly divine attributes are interpreted by Albo in the following ways: First, they are merely explanatory terms of necessary existence,[126] or what Maimonides calls 'names'.[127] Second, they are negations.[128] Third, they are actions.[129] Fourth, they are external relations, these being admissible.[130] But by arguments not unlike those employed by Crescas he is compelled by force of the fourth condition of necessary existence, namely, indeficiency, to omit the existence of essential positive attributes.[131] The compatibility of such attributes with unity is explained by him in a way which is again reminiscent of that of Crescas's explanation. Attributes, he says, have two aspects, in one of which they appear as perfections, and in the other as imperfections. Imperfections they are when they are acquired and in any way separable from the essence. They are pure perfections when they are innate in the

---

[124] *Ikkarim*. [125] Cf. II, 7. [126] Cf. II, 6 and 21.
[127] Cf. *Moreh*, I, 61. [128] Cf. *Ikkarim*, II, 10, 23, and 24.
[129] Cf. *ibid.*, II, 8. [130] Cf. *ibid.*
[131] Cf. *ibid.*, II, 21.

essence and inseparable from it. In God they are inseparable parts of His essence, and, therefore, they are pure perfections and likewise not subversive of His unity. That these pure perfections were not considered by him as identical with the essence, but rather essential to it, is quite clear from the context of his discussion, and that he was here consciously following Crescas may be inferred from his following conclusion: 'Note this well', he says, 'for it is a correct and true interpretation, and one which had been adopted by conservative theologians both ancient and modern.'[132] By ancient he undoubtedly refers to Saadia, and by modern he could not have meant anybody but Crescas, for Gersonides' reputation was not that of a conservative.

Joseph Albo, however, is inconsistent. Having accepted Crescas's explanation that inseparable attributes are not incompatible with divine unity, he rejects the same in the case of existence and unity. In a passage which has been entirely misunderstood by the Hebrew commentators he makes the following statement: 'The meaning of existence in its application to all created beings is by some philosophers taken to be accidental, while by others it is taken as something essential.' Now, the Hebrew commentators have understood this passage to refer to the Avicennean and the Averroesean controversy, 'something essential' thus meaning 'something identical with the essence'.[133] This is, however, manifestly wrong. By 'something essen-

---

[132] Cf. *ibid.*

[133] Cf. *ibid.*, II, 1, and the commentary שרשים *ad loc.* The difficulties of this interpretation have been pointed out in a note (הגה״ה) which appears in the latest undated Wilna edition. The author of that note, too, has failed to see that Albo's reference is to the controversy between Crescas and the Avicennean group rather than that between the latter and Averroes.

tial' he could not have referred to anything but Crescas's theory, which reference alone can be construed with the rest of the text. After thus stating Avicenna's and Crescas's views with regard to the meaning of existence in its ordinary application, Albo proceeds as follows: 'But the term existence in its application to God cannot be accidental, for God is not subject to accidents, as will be demonstrated in the ninth chapter of this part, nor can it be something essential and superadded to its essence, for in this case the divine being would consist of two elements, which is impossible, as will be brought out in the fifth chapter of this part. Consequently existence in the case of God cannot be anything but identical with His essence.' The implication of this passage is clear. Crescas's interpretation of existence as an essential and inseparable condition of essence is discarded by Albo on the ground of its conflict with unity. Albo thus reverses his own position on the other attributes.

In our analysis of Moses Halavi's theory of divine attributes in a previous chapter, we have shown that the attributes to him are mere inventions of the mind, and thus while he interprets divine predicates positively, he does not admit the existence of divine attributes. Yet Crescas endeavours to show that Halavi, too, had believed in the existence of essential attributes. He proves his point indirectly, as an inference of Halavi's theory as to the emanation of plurality from unity. In order to be able fully to understand and appraise the force of Crescas's reasoning, let us give a brief analysis of the nature of the problem of emanation.

Assuming as an axiomatic truth that God is absolute simplicity, and that a simple cause can generate only a simple effect,[134] the question arises as to the origin of the plurality of elements that we observe in the universe. The answer to this question is based upon a combination of Plotinus's theory of emanation and Aristotle's theory of the spheres. There is God, the Absolute One, the Necessarily Existent, or by whatever other name He may be designated, whose knowledge of Himself, being a generative principle, produces the first intelligence. This Intelligence, says Alfarabi, consists of two generative elements, one due to its knowledge of God, and the other due to its knowledge of itself, the former producing the Second Intelligence, and the latter producing the outermost sphere.[135] Alfarabi's statement of the solution is correct in principle, but it is too general to account for the different elements of which the celestial spheres are supposed to be composed. For, according to the early Arabic philosophers, and Avicenna in particular, each sphere is composed, like the sublunar elements, of Matter and Form, and is endowed with a Soul, which is the efficient cause of its motion, and is presided over by an Intelligence, which is the final cause of the same. In Avicenna's statement of the solution, therefore, the self-knowledge of the First Intelligence is declared to contain as many elements as are necessary to explain all the component parts of the spheres. Avicenna's statement is variously reproduced in subsequent works. According to Sharastāni, the reflection of the First Intelligence of his own spiritual essence produces the Form as well as the Soul of the First Sphere, the latter being

[134] As for the origin of this proposition, see Munk, *Mélanges*, p. 361; *Guide*, II, 22, p. 172, note 1; Steinschneider, *Al-Farabi*, p. 9, note 20; Kaufmann, *Attributenlehre*, p. 371, note 11.

[135] Cf. Alfarabi's ספר ההתחלות הנמצאות,
השניים . . . ישכיל הראשון וישכיל עצמותו.

nothing but the consummation of the former, whereas the existence of that Intelligence being mere possibility, produces the matter of the sphere.[136] Algazali's restatement of the case in his *Destruction of the Philosophers* is similar to that of Sharastani's, but, unlike the latter, he maintains that the self-knowledge of the First Intelligence would only account for the Soul of the Sphere, and consequently criticizes Avicenna for his failure to account for the origin of its Form.[137] In all these restatements, the origin of the Second Intelligence is said to be due, as is said by Alfarabi, to the reflection of the First Intelligence of God. In his *Intentions of the Philosophers*, however, Algazali gives a somewhat different and rather inadequate version of the case. The First Intelligence, he says, has two aspects. It is necessary existence in so far as it must come into being through its cause, but it is only possible existence when it is considered with respect to itself. Its necessary aspect, therefore, produces the Second Intelligence, whereas its possible aspect produces the First Sphere.[138] Abraham Ibn Daud, in his *Sublime Faith*, finds three elements in the First Intelligence, from which proceed the Second Intelligence, the First Sphere and its soul.[139] But curiously enough he does not state what these three elements are. Maimonides is probably following Alfarabi, naming only two elements in the First Intelligence, its knowledge of itself which produces the sphere and its knowledge of God which produces the Second Intelligence, and, like Algazali, he argues that this explanation does not account for the

---

[136] Cf. *Sharastani*, pp. 380-81 (Cureton's edition).
[137] Cf. Algazali's *Destruction of the Philosophers*, Disputation III.
[138] Cf. Algazali's *Intentions*, Metaphysics, V.
[139] Cf. *Emunah Ramah*, II, IV, 3.

component parts of the spheres.[140] Joseph Ibn Aknin, in his special treatise on the subject,[141] finds in the First Intelligence three elements: knowledge of God, knowledge of self, and knowledge of its being mere possible existence. The restatement of the case in later Hebrew works are unimportant, as they all follow secondary Hebrew authorities.

It is significant that in all the statements cited the knowledge of God on the part of the First Intelligence is referred to as one of the component parts, the most important one, producing the Second Intelligence. None of these authors, however, specifies what is meant by that knowledge of God, though we may infer that what they meant by it is the knowledge that God is the cause of its existence, since the divine essence itself must be unknowable. Again, the least important element, that which produces the Matter of the Sphere, is designated by them *the mere possibility of existence*.[142] Now, in Moses Halavi's enumeration of the threefold division in the First Intelligence, the first element is, as usual, called the *knowledge of God*,[143] but the third is described as *the knowledge of its being brought into being by the Necessarily Existent*,[144] which, of course, is another way of saying the *knowledge of its mere possible existence*. But in Crescas's paraphrase that expression is changed into *the knowledge of God as its cause and of itself as His effect*.[145] And so Crescas asks, what could Halavi have meant by

---

[140] Cf. *Moreh*, II, 22.

[141] Edited and translated into English by J. L. Magnes (Berlin, 1904).

[142] אפשרות המציאות.

[143] ישכיל מחוייב המציאות.

[144] וישכיל עצמותו שהוא עלול למחוייב המציאות.

[145] ואם מה שישיג היות עצמותו ית' עלה לו והוא עלול ממנו (Crescas's paraphrase, *Or Adonai*, I, III, 3, p. 25 b).

describing the first element as *knowledge of God*? The divine essence itself is unknowable. The comprehension of God as cause is in Crescas's paraphrase of Halavi exactly the phrase by which the third element is described. And to say that it refers to a negative knowledge of God is likewise impossible, since the negative knowledge of God is in its ultimate analysis the knowledge of His causality. Hence it must refer to the knowledge of God's essential attributes, which, concludes Crescas, goes to show that Moses Halavi admitted the existence of essential attributes. And in the same manner it can also be shown that Alfarabi, Avicenna, and Averroes admitted the existence of the same. Averroes, to be sure, rejects the theory of intermediary emanations, believing that all the Intelligences and Spheres emanate directly from the divine essence. Still, contends Crescas, while denying the causal interrelation of the Intelligences, Averroes believes in the presence of some qualitative differentiation between them. That qualitative differentiation must, of course, be due to a corresponding gradation in the simplicity of their comprehension of God. But that comprehension cannot be of the divine essence itself; it must be of the divine attributes, which, therefore, have existence. But, as we have seen, while Averroes admits that the term Intelligence in its application to God is a positive predicate, he is far from believing that it is an essential attribute of God in the same sense as it is understood by Crescas.

Let us now summarize the results we have arrived at in our inquiry. The origin of the problem of attributes, we have stated, lies in the incompatibility of four initial assumptions: the logical interpretation of Scriptural phraseology, the reality of logical relations, the antinominalistic view of universals, and the Avicennean definition of absolute simplicity. We have seen how the various attempts to solve the problem tended either to reject one or more of these assumptions, or to find some explanation in accordance with them. The naïve theologians, referred to by Maimonides, rejected the first assumption that the Scriptural predications are logical propositions. Maimonides retains all the four assumptions, and denying the existence of essential attributes in the divine being, interprets the Scriptural predications of God as privative judgements. Averroes, Gersonides, and Halavi, too, deny the existence of essential attributes in the divine being, but accepting a nominalistic view of universals, and therewithal the non-reality of logical relations, interpret the Scriptural predications of God as positive judgements in which subject and predicate are only verbally related. Algazali's criticism of Avicenna aims to disqualify the latter's definition of absolute simplicity, and thereby affirms the existence of essential attributes. Finally, by advancing a new theory of universals, Crescas attempts to show the compatibility of essential attributes and absolute simplicity.

CPSIA information can be obtained
at www.ICGtesting.com
Printed in the USA
LVHW081428200420
654120LV00012B/2151